SUCCESS STORIES

Other Bestselling Books by
Robert T. Kiyosaki & Sharon L. Lechter

Rich Dad Poor Dad
What The Rich Teach Their Kids About Money That The Poor And Middle Class Do Not

Rich Dad's CASHFLOW Quadrant
Rich Dad's Guide To Financial Freedom

Rich Dad's Guide to Investing
What The Rich Invest In That The Poor And Middle Class Do Not

Rich Dad's Rich Kid Smart Kid
Give Your Child A Financial Head Start

Rich Dad's Retire Young Retire Rich
How To Get Rich Quickly And Stay Rich Forever

Rich Dad's Prophecy
Why The Biggest Stock Market Crash In History Is Still Coming...
And How You Can Prepare Yourself And Profit From It!

Rich Dad's Success Stories
Real Life Success Stories from Real Life People
Who Followed the Rich Dad Lesson

SUCCESS
STORIES

By Robert T. Kiyosaki with Sharon L. Lechter, C.P.A.
The Authors of *Rich Dad Poor Dad*

WARNER
BUSINESS
BOOKS™

Published by Warner Books

An AOL Time Warner Company

Copyright © 2003 by Robert T. Kiyosaki and Sharon L. Lechter.
All rights reserved.

Published by Warner Books in association with CASHFLOW Technologies, Inc., and BI Capital, Inc.

CASHFLOW and Rich Dad are registered trademarks of CASHFLOW Technologies, Inc.
Rich Dad's Advisors is a trademark of CASHFLOW Technologies, Inc.

   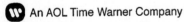

are trademarks of
CASHFLOW Technologies, Inc.

Warner Business Books are published by Warner Books, Inc.,
1271 Avenue of the Americas, New York, NY 10020

Visit our Web sites at www.richdad.com and www.twbookmark.com

An AOL Time Warner Company

The Warner Business Book logo is a trademark of Warner Books, Inc.

Printed in the United States of America

First Printing: October 2003

Library of Congress Cataloging-in-Publication Data

    Rich dad's success stories : real life success stories from real life people who followed the rich dad lessons / [compiled by] Robert T. Kiyosaki and Sharon L. Lechter.
       p. cm.
    ISBN 0-446-69180-1
      1. Finance, Personal.   2. Financial security.   3. Investments.   I. Kiyosaki, Robert T., 1947–
    II. Lechter, Sharon L.
    HG179.R45   2003
    332.024'01—dc21
                                                  2003012326

Contents

Preface by Robert Kiyosaki

I love *Rich Dad's Success Stories* for the following reasons.

1. These people took action and achieved successful results. A few weeks ago, I was on a local television show in Phoenix, Arizona, where Kim and I live. The host was interviewing a reader of *Rich Dad Poor Dad* and me. The reader said that she had liked the book but felt it was a waste of time to read. Her complaint to me, and thousands of TV viewers, was "The book did not tell me what to do next." I did not respond because my blood was boiling. Rather than say anything, I faked a smile and silently nodded.

"So what should she do?" asked the TV host.

"Find another book that will tell her what to do," was my feeble reply.

One of my pet peeves is people who only do things they are told to do. Ever since I was a little kid in school, I noticed that there were classmates of mine who did very well in school, simply by doing what the teacher told them to do. Often they were called the *teacher's pet*. On the other hand, I often did things I was not told to do, or told not to do . . . and that got me in trouble. So early in my life, I realized that I was a person that hated to be told what to do, which is why I do my best to not tell people what to do in my books.

Bookstores and libraries are filled with "how to" books. For people who love to be told how to do something, such books are just for them. Rich Dad books are *not* "how to" books. They are books dedicated to passing on my rich dad's financial wisdom and guidance. They are stories about my own path of trial and error, utilizing rich dad's wisdom, and turning my errors and experiences into my own personal lessons. Never do I expect anyone to follow my path. I simply share my lessons learned along the way and encourage others to find their own path.

Rich Dad books are written for the purpose of expanding the reader's possibilities in life, rather than becoming a specific recipe book on how to get rich. Years ago, my rich dad explained to me that there were millions of ways to get rich. It was my job to find the way that best fit me. So rather than get rich following my rich dad's footsteps, using his recipe for success, I took his guidance and wisdom and found the path that worked best for me. And that is what *this* book is filled with. This book is filled with success stories of people who took rich dad's wisdom and then found their own path to financial success. They are not people sitting around, waiting for someone to tell them what to do next.

There are millions of people today, working at dead-end jobs, working hard, putting money into investments that lose money, many realizing that they may never be able to retire, yet waiting for someone to take them by the hand and show them the way out of their financial trap. Hopefully they will go to a bookstore or library and find the "how to" book that can take them by the hand and show them their way out. The people in this book did not need a "how to" book. Instead, they have written their own "how to" story on how they found their own path to financial success.

2. These people did well financially, while at the same time millions of people lost trillions of dollars. Rich Dad Poor Dad was first published in April of 1997. Some of you may recall that was the era of the dot.com bubble and mania. People who had never invested before were taking money out of the equity in their homes, their savings and putting their hard-earned money into mutual funds, stock, and even IPOs, initial public offerings, generally an investment vehicle reserved only for the rich and financially sophisticated.

While I was on promotional tours between 1997 and 2003, I often warned investors about the perils of the stock market and how risky mutual funds were. On several occasions, I was slammed by financial commentators for criticizing mutual funds and the stock market and on one program was

even asked to leave. Several financial magazines and newpapers openly crit-
icized my book and my rich dad's message. Several publications actually
published lies and false statements about me, in an attempt to discredit me,
and my rich dad's message. Beginning in 2003, however, many of these same
financial commentators had started acknowledging that the Rich Dad message has great merit.

Today after millions of people have lost trillions of dollars, it is indeed a
pleasure to read a book about people who did well financially during this extremely turbulent financial era. I am also certain there are many people, including those commentators, who wish they had followed my rich dad's advice
rather than their financial planner's advice during this same time period.

3. Rich dad's lessons and wisdom do work. I still hear people saying,
"I'm waiting for the market to come back." I also see financial advisors who
gave bad advice before the market crash still handing out the same bad advice after the crash. They're still saying, "Invest for the long term, diversify,
buy and hold." They also continue to say, "The market goes up on average 9
percent per year." The sad thing is that there are still millions of investors
who continue to heed that advice, even though there is overwhelming evi-
dence that the advice did not work. How people can continue to follow bad
advice or, even worse, get paid for handing out such bad financial advice is
beyond me. This book is about some people who took control and took responsibility for their own financial education and their financial future. Rich
dad often said, "The reason so many people do not do well financially is because they take financial advice from salespeople, not rich people."

The Real Reason I Love This Book

Of these three main reasons I love this book, a book about real-life people
becoming financially successful in the real world, the first one is the most important.

It is because these people took action. We ended *Rich Dad Poor Dad,* our
first book, with "Take Action," and these people did. They took risks. More
importantly, they took responsibility for their own financial education and
their financial future. They did not simply turn their money over to a large financial institution and hope and pray that the large financial institution had
their best interest at heart, which is what millions of people are still doing.

We are heading into an era of great financial turmoil and uncertainty. The financial storms that lie ahead will test all of us . . . me included. The people in this book who shared their stories are better prepared today to be able to handle the financial storms of tomorrow. Because they took action, learned, gained experience and wisdom, and succeeded, they are better prepared for the future, and that is what I am most excited about. The future will be very bright for those that are preparing today. Unfortunately, the future may be very grim for those who are waiting for the good old days of the past to return to the future.

ROBERT KIYOSAKI

Taking Action with Rich Dad by Sharon Lechter

In *Rich Dad's CASHFLOW Quadrant* we introduced the CASHFLOW Quadrant, which describes the four types of people in the financial world.

The E and the S on the left side of the Quadrant represent employee and self-employed or small business owner. Typically the employee is looking for job security and benefits, while the S is a specialist and ends up "owning" his or her job. The more successful they become, the busier they are and the more tied to their job or business. The left side is the side that our traditional school prepares you for. It is also referred to as the "rat race."

The B and I on the right side of the Quadrant represent the business owner and investor. The business owner has other people work for him or her and has defined systems by which the business operates. It operates independently of the owner. The investor has his or her money working for him or her. In review, financial freedom is found on the right side of the CASHFLOW Quadrant. We also refer to the right side as the "fast track."

The people who share their success stories in this book all want to achieve a similar goal: financial freedom. They are all striving to move to the right side of the Quadrant. When we hear from our readers, they almost always talk about shifting from the left side of the CASHFLOW Quadrant to the right side. No one ever tells us they are going in the opposite direction. That's because they have recognized that moving from the left side of the CASHFLOW Quadrant to the right side is the way to achieve financial independence.

Rich dad teaches that on the right side of the Quadrant is where your money works hard for you. Many times people tell us they are bridging the quadrants, with one foot in the E or S quadrant while owning a business or investing in real estate on the right side. Their goal is to create enough cashflow so that they can leave their job or S quadrant life and live totally on the right side as a business owner and investor.

Their stories tell the difference between being totally dependent on others for income versus being in control of one's financial life. They share the fears they faced around money and how they learned to overcome that fear as well. As rich dad advised, they developed their own path, one that was right for them.

They took steps to achieving financial security by either buying businesses or investing in real estate or both. People who already own businesses used rich dad's lessons to help them run those businesses in a better, more owner-friendly way.

None of them were money experts before they began their financial education. Some hold advanced degrees from noted universities; others just made it through high school. A few are still in school. It doesn't matter what kind of education they received, they now all understand the importance of acquiring assets and knowing the difference between good debt and bad debt. No matter what their personal circumstances were, what country they lived in, or how they started financially, they all learned the most important aspects of cashflow, took charge of their financial lives, and are well on their path to financial freedom. Several of them have left the rat race and are living happily on the right side of the Quadrant, the fast track. If, like the people in the book, you have found financial success through rich dad's lessons, please share your stories with us at www.richdad.com, so others may be inspired by your success.

You Can Take Charge, Too

If you've ever felt deep down inside that working as an employee or being self-employed wasn't giving you the financial security you craved, there is an alternative. If your investments have lost value, you are tired of the same old financial advice, you worry about ever being able to retire, or you just want to spend more time with your family, the way to financial freedom can be found. This book is filled with success stories of people who took rich dad's wisdom and then found their own path to financial success.

You can create your own Rich Dad success story.

Best wishes as you find your own path to financial success,
SHARON LECHTER

Part I

It's How You Play the Game

If you want to achieve financial security, you'll need to learn the game of money. I learned the game of money from my rich dad. From my Rich Dad's lessons I created the board game CASHFLOW. This game teaches you financial skills through fun, repetition, and action. It is so unique that it has been awarded patents. It will challenge you, teach you, and require you to think like rich people think. The people in this section describe their financial successes and attribute those achievements to playing the CASH-FLOW games.

These people discovered that unlike all kinds of other board games that can be won only one way and only during the time in which the game is played, CASHFLOW provided lessons that go long past the playing time. Every time these people participated in the game not only did they increase their financial skills they built up their confidence as well. Using the deal cards, they told me, offered new ways to think about investments. The deal cards, which gave them different options each time they played, provided information for starting cashflow-producing investments.

For Ed and Terry Colman, who live in California, the deal cards that motivated them were about real estate. Their journey to financial security will likely strike a chord with many. If you lived through the 1960s, as they did, you might have also been influenced by the hippie era in which financial success was not a goal. Actually, the opposite situation was the ultimate quest: Live free, forget about money, and do your own thing. Focusing on the future was regarded as a waste of time.

Ed and Terry are refreshingly honest about their past view of money. Like a lot of people of their generation, they played into the mood of the times and scorned financial matters. What they earned, they spent. Planning for the future just wasn't a consideration (at least not until their son, Jake, whose story also appears in this book, was born).

When they realized that they needed a financial plan, they began to explore different options. Some worked, some didn't. But they didn't give up. They continued to learn because they wanted to find a way to financial freedom. Eventually they saw that investing in real estate offered them excellent opportunities to do that. You'll see what they did and how they did it and follow the small steps they took that led to even bigger and bigger ones.

If you're a baby boomer who has lost touch with his or her finances and thinks it's too late to get on a new track, read what the Colmans have to say. It's never too late to change your mind about becoming wealthy—especially when you have found the means to help you do it.

But if you're in your thirties, facing big debt, and very worried about whether financial security will ever be yours, read Tracey Rodriguez's story. Like many people forced to declare bankruptcy, Tracey and her husband were in a difficult predicament. Hard workers, they were nonetheless forced into a tough financial situation. For them, financial security is now rooted in owning businesses, which were also inspired by the CASHFLOW game deal cards.

Perhaps you're in your fifties, and believe that creating cashflow investments isn't for you. I've heard people in this age group say negative things like, "It's too late for me," "I'm too tired to do that," and "I'm too old to change." If that's what you believe, then read what Cecilia Morrison has to say about changing perspective. For Cecilia, and her husband, George, retirement will be funded by steady cashflow because a deal card from CASHFLOW motivated her to make new investments.

How Ed and Terry, Tracey and Cecilia have taken control of their financial lives are stories of coming to terms with reality and making choices. The decisions they have made—and continue to make—are exciting. As these people achieve financial security, they are winners as they play the game of life.

Chapter 1

Money Matters

ED AND TERRY COLMAN
Venice, California

If we watched a movie about 1960s free thinkers morphing into twenty-first-century rent collectors we would have chalked it up as a Hollywood fantasy. But the story is true. Three years ago, Terry and I began to buy real estate. We now own eight homes in three states worth over $1 million.

How and why we changed our minds and moved from fiscal stagnation to financial action is, in a very profound way, the story of how many in our generation have changed, too.

Take One

Maybe our pre–real estate situation shouldn't have been so surprising. Money had not been a topic of discussion in my house, so I didn't receive any information, much less training, about it. My parents thought I was irresponsible where money was concerned; as soon I got it, I spent it. In contrast, my younger sister, the "responsible one," always saved her money.

Education was regarded as a good thing, but I was never told that I needed to get a good education that would lead to a solid job and that I'd be set for life. In order to be a well-rounded person, education was necessary. My sister graduated from college, but after three years at Antioch College, I left school.

While I was growing up in Los Angeles, Terry was across the country in New York. Still, she racked up two years of college in California. We met in 1980, married in 1987, and both of us stayed rooted in the hippie mode of the 1960s and 1970s.

We held on to the conviction that money, the currency of "filthy capitalist pigs," wasn't important. Many in our generation embraced a righteous indignation where money was concerned. Living check to check seemed natural and the ambition to accumulate a lot of money never bit us. "Free love" was the currency of our generation. We knew nothing about finance and we weren't inclined to learn.

Fifteen years ago, when we were in our thirties, we worked in the motion picture production business. I was an assistant cameraman who kind of fell into the industry. My father, a freelance cameraman and director, had asked me if I wanted to give the job a try. My background was in graphic arts and photography and since I wasn't really doing anything at the time I said sure. I didn't see this as a particularly great opportunity or a step on a much desired career path. Work just meant money.

One day Terry came to the set where I was working and noticed the makeup specialist's efforts. The skill appealed to her, and she became a makeup artist, as well as a hand model.

We were hired to do a lot of commercials, which entailed travel and hotels and a rather glamorous lifestyle. Sure, we worked job to job and put in fifteen-hour days, ten or twenty days a month, but the rest of the time was ours. We went to the beach and when we wanted to play tennis that's what we did. Spending money was the goal. We had a great time living moment to moment.

On the surface, this was a very "free" and cool way to live but the reality changed the moment our son, Jake, was born almost fourteen years ago. His arrival was a loud wake-up call. With no plan for the future, we never considered what would happen to us—much less to our son—ten or twenty years hence. We carried more than $10,000 in credit card debt and counted less than $500 in our savings account. We had no goals, no assets, no investments, and no way out of the dire predicament we found ourselves in. "What do we do now?" we asked ourselves.

Terry stayed home with Jake while I worked. Unfortunately, my schedule was crazy. Sometimes I'd be gone for weeks at a time. By the time Jake was old enough to notice I wasn't home and would ask "Where's Dad?" we felt trapped. I couldn't leave the film business. It was what I knew and I couldn't imagine working in any other field even if anyone would hire me. We knew we had to make changes, but where to start?

It was time to grow up.

Take Two

Let me set the scene for you. By 1992, Terry and I, ready to act on our financial future, were willing to try something different. One sunny California morning, I was in a park, pushing Jake in a swing. Another dad was doing likewise. Already there was something different about this day because two dads entertaining their kids at a park on a weekday was unusual.

We began to talk and the man told me he was with the Amway business, which deals with network marketing. It turned out that his sponsorship was in Hawaii, a place both Terry and I loved. When Terry met him and heard about the Hawaiian connection her response was purely emotional. Here was a way for us to get back to Hawaii. We did much more than that.

We started to build our own organization but we didn't create a huge downline, that is, sponsor other people in the organization. But something very valuable did come out of this venture. Just when we were ready for it, we learned how to do business. The procedure training seminars, instructions on how to present the plan, sales training, and reading lists containing personal development and success principle books provided us with a terrific learning experience and spurred tremendous personal growth. We started to associate with successful people we could learn from. Mingling with millionaires who shared their wisdom unlocked our minds and cast out our narrow views about finance. How money could be used—in addition to how the world of money worked—was a mind-expanding experience.

The suggested book list was particularly valuable. *The Richest Man in Babylon* really opened our eyes to the way we were dealing with money. Two years after reading that book all our credit card debt had been eliminated and our savings account held thousands of dollars. *How to Win Friends and Influence People* was another enormously important book for us. Reading it gave us the tools to deal with others effectively.

Being in the right place at the right time—in this instance the swing set at the park—led to business training. Now we had graduated from the first phase of our financial education. What, we wondered, were we supposed to do next?

Take Three

Six years ago I became self-employed when I established a service business. We, along with six independent contractors who worked project by project, supervised the transfer of film to videotape for commercial production companies. Originally I had a partner, who I subsequently bought out in the spring of 2000. With no investment capital to tap into, we ran the business from a tiny back bedroom in our house for the first four years. A computer, fax machine, cell phone, and pager were all we needed to get started. Carrying low overhead was a clear decision and we were pleased with our virtual office, where a twenty-four-hour service outside the house handled our calls. A real person answered the phone with the name of our business, took the message, and paged me. I returned the call right away.

I took care of everything from sales and billing to scheduling, from training to mailing out holiday cards. Doing the bulk of supervising the session was also my responsibility. It was exhausting.

A couple of years ago we hired a part-time office person to take over the day-to-day operating functions such as billing and data entry. But even with the roster of associates, who supervised the sessions, I found that I was still required to make a lot of the daily decisions regarding scheduling, personnel, and finances. The question I heard more than any other was, "What do you want me to do about . . ."

Hitching a ride on the dot.com express, we took advantage of the advertising dollars available. We did well and figured that we should take advantage of the boom that was taking place in the stock market.

Take Four

After my grandparents died and left me a few thousand dollars, we invested the money in mutual funds. Five years ago, thinking we were finally taking control of our financial destiny, we converted our mutual funds to individual stock positions.

During the first two years of "investing," our portfolio grew pretty much no matter what we did or bought. At one point it rose 30 percent overall. Over a period of three years, our investments, which included five IRA accounts, totaled $80,000. After doing some rudimentary research we thought we picked solid, reliable companies. We bought shares in companies such as AT&T, Dell, General Electric, DuPont, Kodak, GM, Berkshire Hathaway, Microsoft, Lucent, WorldCom, and a few smaller riskier stocks as well.

Complacent, I didn't monitor our portfolio nearly enough. Nor did I follow closely the financial information the companies were sending me. I didn't possess the education to invest in stocks safely—for instance no trailing stops, that is, an order to automatically sell a stock if it goes below a certain price, were in place. Without an advisor to provide accurate information and insight, we put our money and ourselves in a precarious position.

When the market started to collapse in 2000, I wasn't paying attention. A few months went by and when I next looked at our portfolio it was down between 30 percent and 40 percent. Still I did nothing because I was waiting for the market to recover. I hadn't done my homework, and still hung on to the long-term buy-and-hold mentality. It was a big mistake.

Now our total stock portfolio value is about $46,000, which represents almost a 50 percent loss. This experience taught us a tough lesson. To be successful in any investment strategy, one needs to access correct and current information and constantly monitor the situation. It is also vital to hire an advisor one trusts.

The old saying applies: When the student is ready, the teacher appears.

Visiting a friend's home four years ago, we noticed a copy *Rich Dad Poor Dad* sitting on the kitchen counter. I admit that I didn't immediately react to it although Terry picked up on it right away. She bought a copy and we started reading it.

Three years ago, after we began playing CASHFLOW 101, we attended a seminar on Veterans Administration (VA) foreclosures. The seminar provided a network of brokers and agents in place to help students buy these homes. All were small deals type of housing. When we saw the financial breakdowns, they looked exactly like one of the small deal cards from the game. We said, "Hey, this is a small deal card. We have been doing them for months in the kitchen, why not do it now for real?"

Here's How We Did It

We went to the Internet and, based on the information we received at the seminar, began searching for properties. VA foreclosures required a bid, with the highest bidder winning. They also came with a predetermined mortgage rate. These loans, which were all conventional thirty-year fixed rate mortgages, were very easy to qualify for. When we began buying real estate the rate was 8 percent and over time it dropped by increments to 6 percent.

Initially, our focus was on southern Florida and the Phoenix area so we contacted real estate agents in Port St. Lucie, a bedroom community of Palm Beach, as well as in Phoenix. Our reasoning was this: We were interested in the lowest cash investment required, and those two states qualified. (Each state within the VA program has slightly different parameters. For example, in Florida the VA requires $1,000 down to buy property. In Arizona, the amount is 5 percent of the bid price.)

The Phoenix real estate agent mailed us packets of available VA properties, including photos, along with a breakdown of purchase costs, suggested bids, management fees, expenses, taxes, insurance, estimated repairs, and net cashflow.

The agent in Florida put the same information up on his Web site.

We looked at several properties and analyzed the numbers that were provided. Then we played with them with the help of a financial calculator (we bought ours in Staples for about $50). The aim was to determine the maximum amount we were willing to bid and still receive a positive cashflow. When we found a property that we liked, we would put in a bid based on our calculations. If our price won, we were delighted. If we lost it, we didn't care because we weren't willing to pay more for the property.

After making a few bids but losing, we had a winner. This particular three-bedroom, two-bath single-family house in Port St. Lucie was priced at $98,000. Our credit was good, so we knew we would qualify for the loan with no trouble and we knew that we could use money from our savings and stock sales to cover repairs, the down payment, and the closing costs. The fix-up took a few weeks and our agent had a tenant standing by to move in within thirty days.

Here's the breakdown of what we did:

Cash invested into property

Down payment:	$1,000
Closing costs paid by us:	$3,000
Repairs/renovations paid by us:	$3,900
	$7,900

Monthly cashflow analysis

Rental income:	$1,040
— Vacancy loss (the house has never been vacant):	$0
Total income:	$1,040
Monthly expenses:	
— Taxes (property) and insurance:	$267
— Repairs/maintenance:	$25
— Reserve:	$25
— Management fee:	$45
— Loan payment (30 years at 8%):	$711
	$1,073
Net monthly cashflow:	($33)

Yes, owing $33 sounds like we were going in the wrong direction, since we had no cashflow for such a big outlay of time and energy. But to us it represented the potential for financial independence. *The indisputable fact was that we owned an income property that our tenant was going to pay for.* Recently we refinanced the loan at 6.125 percent, which reduced our monthly loan payment to $579. Here are our revised monthly cashflow numbers:

Monthly rent:	$1,040
— Monthly expenses:	$941
Monthly cashflow:	$99
Cash-on-cash return	
Annual cashflow ($99 × 12)	$1,188
÷	
Amount of cash put into property	$7,900
Cash-on-cash return	15%

(Try getting that from a bank!)

We closed on this house in October 2000. In that time the prices for properties in Port St. Lucie have skyrocketed. The house was recently appraised at $126,000, a 23 percent increase in value. Our initial investment of $7,900 bought an asset in which we have $26,000 worth of equity (the appraised value minus what is left to pay on the loan). If we sold the house today for $126,000, then that's a whopping 329 percent return, excluding annual cashflow.

"Wow," we said to each other. "We can do this again." And that's what we did, repeating the same process. Something wonderful was happening. By converting earnings and paper "assets" to true assets that were providing cashflow and equity, we were taking control of our lives in a totally new way. Excited and motivated, over the next two years we won the bids on three more properties, one in Clarksville, Tennessee, and two more in Port St. Lucie.

Because one of the Port St. Lucie homes was not financed by the VA, we had to find our own financing. Through the agent in Florida we contacted a loan agent for a local bank. We qualified for a conventional loan with an interest rate of 6.75 percent with 5 percent down. Because the VA was not financing this house, the number of bidders dropped, and our bid of $60,600 won the three-bedroom, two-bathroom home. Here's the breakdown:

Cash put into property

Down payment:	$3,030
Closing costs paid by us:	$3,000
Repairs/renovations paid by us:	$5,000
	$11,030

Monthly cashflow analysis

Rental income:	$825
– Vacancy loss (5%):	$41.25
Total income:	$783.75

Monthly expenses:	
– Taxes (property) and insurance:	$186
– Repairs:	$25
– Maintenance:	$25
– Reserve:	$25
– Management fee (5% of rents):	$41.25
– Loan payment (30 years at 6.75%):	$375
	$677.25
Net monthly cashflow:	$106.50

Cash-on-cash return

Annual cashflow ($106.50 × 12)	$1,278
÷	
Amount of cash put into property	$11,030
Cash-on-cash return:	11.6%

We closed on the property in December 2000. This house, based on similar properties in the area, is worth about $82,000—and that's a conservative estimate.

We located a single-family VA home in Tennessee, again over the Internet, for $500 down on a price of $78,000. This time, the agent, who sent us pictures of several homes, had a harder time finding a tenant. The fix-up costs, which came to nearly $3,000, were more than anticipated and the taxes were higher than estimated. When he finally found a tenant a couple of months later, the house had a net negative cashflow of $40. We also didn't like the way the management was handled. When this house appreciates enough in value, we will sell it. We are also looking at other ways we can turn this house into a positive cashflow property.

We went on to buy another VA foreclosure in Phoenix, this time at a purchase price of $118,500. Here's the breakdown:

Cash put into property

Down payment:	$5,925
Closing costs paid by us:	$4,000
Repairs/renovations paid by us:	$3,000
	$12,925

Monthly cashflow analysis

Rental income:	$1,050
– Vacancy loss (5%):	$52.50
Total income:	$997.50

Monthly expenses:	
– Taxes (property) and insurance:	$121
– Repairs:	$0
– Maintenance:	$25
– Reserve:	$25
– Management fee (5% of rents):	$52.50
– Loan payment (30 years at 8%):	$826
	$1,049.50
Net monthly cashflow:	($52)

Cash-on-cash return

Annual cashflow ($52 × 12)	($624)
÷	
Amount put into property	$12,925
Cash-on-cash return	(5%)

Even with this slightly negative cashflow property, our tenant is still buying our asset for us, and we have enough income from our other investments to cover costs and maintenance. Today similar properties in the area are selling for $128,000.

When we went to look at it, the real estate agent showed us a new development that was being built and we snapped up a new house that was under construction for $127,500 with 5 percent ($6,350) down. We based our decision on the word of this guy that it was in a good, rapidly appreciating area. However, once the house was completed, it sat vacant for months because the agent, who was also with the management company, was unable to rent it. Management, we learned, was a key factor to the success of our real estate empire. We were recommended to another management company, which was able to rent the new home within a month. The monthly cashflow is $75.

Recently the VA foreclosure program has become so popular, and the loan so attractive, that bids have risen and consequently cashflow has eroded. Sometimes, cashflow projections are negative instead of positive. Because we want positive cashflow properties, we've turned to other options. The agent in Florida is now connected with a developer of new homes. We bought one last year with our own financing. The builder recommended his loan program and he was willing to discount the price of the three-bedroom, two-bathroom house if we used his lender. We qualified for the loan and went ahead with the deal, purchasing the house for $102,750 with 5 percent down. The builder picked up the $3,000 closing costs. The advantage of a new home, of course, is that there is no need for fix-up. Also, maintenance is minimal. Here's the breakdown:

Cash put into property

Down payment:	$5,137
Closing costs paid by us:	$1,563
Repairs/renovations paid by us:	$0
	$6,700

Monthly cashflow analysis

Rental income:	$1,090
— Vacancy loss (the house has never been vacant):	$0
Total income:	$1,090
Monthly expenses:	
— Taxes (property) and insurance:	$350
— Repairs and maintenance:	$25
— Reserve:	$25
— Management fee (5% of rents):	$54.50
— Loan payment (30 years at 6.275%):	$609
	$1,063.50
Net monthly cashflow:	$26.50

Cash-on-cash return

Annual cashflow ($26.50 × 12)	$318
÷	
Amount put into property	$6,700
Cash-on-cash return	4.7%

Today similar properties in the area are selling for $126,000. We are currently buying another one of these new homes.

The monthly cashflow on our first seven properties is $324. Our equity totals nearly $130,000 with an initial cash investment of approximately $60,000, which includes closing costs and repairs. That's an average cash-on-cash return of 7 percent, *excluding appreciation and tax advantages.* Plus, and this is the most important part, *the tenants are buying our assets for us!* Here's the "magic" formula we use: Borrow the money to buy assets and have someone else pay it back.

Take Six

We have learned from Rich Dad that real estate is the road to financial freedom. As our financial education continues, we:

• Know how to analyze a property to determine if it is or is not a good deal.

• Understand that management is the key to long-term property success. Good management can make a good deal great. Bad management can make a good deal marginal and a marginal deal bad.

• Seek out and surround ourselves with like-minded people. Those who shoot themselves in a symbolic foot with negative comments like, "I'll never be able to do that," "That's too expensive," and "Why bother?" are manufacturing excuses for not trying. We choose not to be in their orbit because they drag us down.

• Are learning about what bankers will lend and why and when they will not.

• Are also finding out that buying a property is not an emotional experience based on how we respond to how the place looks. We haven't seen most of the houses in person; we can't drive by them to check them out, so there is an intangible quality to our ownership. The cashflow, however, is concrete.

One of the biggest changes in our lives concerns risk. Before Rich Dad, my definition of taking chances revolved around the physical challenges of mountain climbing. Now we define inaction as being risky. Continuing on a path that goes nowhere and pouring money into investments over which one has no control is as foolhardy as scaling a mountain without the right equipment.

The other huge change involved my tendency to procrastinate. I'm combating my laziness simply by doing that which I need to do, even though I might not like it. The first four years of our service business, people came to me. Now I have to pursue them aggressively. I don't enjoy calling people I don't know but I know I must do it, for work and for real estate investing.

The notion of lack of time or that I wouldn't act fast enough to achieve my goals was tough for me. But because Rich Dad simplified complex concepts and presented them in a very easy-to-understand manner, I calmed down. With a continuing financial education at my disposal I know we can achieve what we want to do.

My business remains in the S or self-employed cashflow quadrant. It could run in my absence but it wouldn't grow without my participation. The truth is, it tends to shrink without my constant input. Currently we're exploring strategies to move it into a B business. One possibility would be licensing facilities in other cities. In order to obtain the free time I want to develop and oversee my real estate investments, this business must be able to run on its own.

Within the next year we intend to buy our first multifamily property, either by ourselves or with a partner. Our five-year goal is to raise our monthly passive income to $10,000 a month. When that happens I will retire from our business and officially exit the rat race. We won't depend on $1,000 a month from Social Security. Millions of dollars' worth of real estate will fund the rest of our lives.

That's a Wrap

We often felt trapped in the present and uncertain about the future. And while the future holds many unknowns, we maintain a far better idea of what is coming and how to prepare for it. We feel that we're in the midst of a journey, and success is part of the process of getting from where we are now to where we are going. With growing confidence in our increased financial knowledge, we feel that we are doing the right thing for us and for our son. A reality more satisfying than any movie ending, the ultimate goal of reaching financial freedom is ahead.

We feel very proud of ourselves. We look at ourselves, acknowledge how far we've come, know we are learning more every day, and take stock of what we already did and what we plan to do. Unlike our younger, more naive selves, we made a conscious decision to find out how the world works, to be open to change, and to be responsible for our financial well-being. And we're breathing a whole lot easier where retirement is concerned.

We always thought of ourselves as being enormously wealthy; now our financial assets are finally catching up with us.

Chapter 2

We Mind Our Own Businesses

Tracey Rodriguez
Phoenix, Arizona

Ten years ago, while just in our twenties, we were forced to declare bankruptcy, a scary and extremely unpleasant predicament to be in. The story of how we went from receiving twenty calls a day demanding money for eight months to collecting passive income involves two opposites. One was the circumstance beyond our control. The other was the circumstance we decided to take control of, thanks to Rich Dad.

My husband, David, and I own three businesses that are still growing and count a rental property as an asset as well. We live in a nice house and drive good cars—and our family and friends take us a little more seriously than they used to do.

A Familiar Story

When I was growing up in San Diego, California, my family existed from paycheck to paycheck although I didn't know that at the time. We lived in a beautiful home where money was never discussed. My parents were divorced and

I lived with my mom and stepfather, who was a firefighter. As a teenager I didn't know that my mom, who worked in an OB-GYN office, saved $20 every payday. At the beginning of every year of high school she would hand me $300 for clothes, a very impressive sum. Christmas time was an excuse for excess spending because my stepfather received a bonus. But money was so tight the rest of the year that I couldn't afford to be a cheerleader.

After I graduated from high school, I began to wonder what it would be like to be my own boss. Those thoughts were put aside as David and I began a new phase of our lives.

In 1991 we were both working year-round at a ski resort and enjoying a very good life. Earning more money than we ever had before, we bought jet skis and snazzy cars. But then we were laid off and, while we got jobs in Reno, we earned less money and found ourselves playing catch-up with our bills.

Then, in 1992, I became pregnant. When my doctor ordered me to stay in bed for three months the company I worked for let me go. My premature daughter was born the day before Thanksgiving. Very soon we were over $50,000 in debt from medical bills and the old bills we still owed. With no other choices available to us we sold the jet skis and the cars. Then we declared bankruptcy. I was twenty-four years old.

But I still held on to my dream that someday I could be my own boss. I attended a trade school and become a cosmetologist. At the same time I was the representative for a lingerie line. David worked, too. We had another baby.

Outwardly we were taking care of our responsibilities and looking after our children. But inwardly I felt like less of a person. There were dark, panicky moments when I thought to myself, "How am I ever going to face anything again?" Our stained credit history followed us for ten long years.

But still we persevered. In 1993 we joined a multilevel marketing business and in 1996 spun off a promotion business of our own. But how we handled that business, and everything that was to come after, turned around in 2001 when a mentor, who was involved with the promotion business, introduced me to the Rich Dad books.

The Red Ink Turns Black

When I began reading *Rich Dad Poor Dad* I was working as a bar manager at a resort hotel in North Scottsdale, Arizona. I would carry the book to the bar and read it between pouring drinks. Everything I wanted to accomplish—owning a business, becoming wealthy, gaining personal freedom—but didn't know how to do, was there. The specific education I needed to get me where I wanted to go was in my hands.

Because I'm a member of the Phoenix Convention and Visitors Bureau I had the opportunity to attend one of Robert and Kim's seminars. They were kind enough to autograph a copy of Rich Dad's *Retire Young, Retire Rich* and then actually invited me to their office to play CASHFLOW 101. Surprised and grateful, I took them up on their generous offer.

With this new information at hand, I started to see my life in another way. Before I always had a really tough time motivating myself to get through the hard times. More than once I would just sit in a chair and do nothing because I couldn't summon up the energy to get myself moving.

But now I realized that an inspiring resource was always with me, whenever I needed it. Knowledge and guidance supported me whenever I wanted to move forward. Knowing this, my confidence jumped and I was able to overcome the triple self-imposed barriers I had constructed for myself: believing that my limited education would hold me back, thinking I had no time to make changes, and fearing what others thought about me. I began to conquer all the obstacles Robert wrote about: cynicism, laziness, bad habits, arrogance, and, especially, fear.

I always wanted to look good at what I was doing and not appear foolish. I was afraid of picking up a phone and making an appointment, wondering, "How can I do this?" Fear of failing was the worst of all. But now the fears began to fade. The shadow of the bankruptcy receded. I began to buy businesses that spin off passive monthly income.

Here's How I Did It

A shaved ice business, which we bought in 2002, produces a positive cashflow of $1,500 a month. We sell Tropical Icy Treats and Snow Cones and we're planning to expand to selling other kinds of snacks.

I thought of this business while playing CASHFLOW 101 at the Rich Dad office for the second time. It was on one of the deal cards that helped me get out of the rat race. Inspired, that very week I checked the newspaper for businesses for sale and sure enough, an ad was listed. Immediately I saw double value: I could handle the business and I knew my family would enjoy it.

To finance the venture, I first asked the seller for an owner finance deal, that is, to finance my first year at 20 percent interest. He was going to do it but when I spoke to one of my mentors, who happens to be a real estate investor, about it he said that he would lend us the money out of his Roth IRA account. We accepted and bought the business for $5,000 with a flat interest rate of 20 percent, with $500, paid back every month for a year. The total cost: $6,000 for the twelve-month period. I decided to have a custom-made cart built, which took about three weeks to make. The cost was included in the $5,000 sale price.

For now David and I run all of the events. We have been doing festivals, craft fairs, and county fairs. Additionally, we have a contract with the city of Avondale to be the snack person at one of their parks—it's called Freedom Park and I love that name—every Tuesday, Wednesday, and Thursday night.

The goal is to do so for one year to learn the ins and outs of the business, which right now is licensed only in Arizona. (The license fee was included when we purchased the cart.) At that point we'll hire people to run it for us.

For the four months that we've owned the stand, we've taken in over $1,000 a month. That gives us $500 a month in passive cashflow because we're still paying back $500 a month on the loan. The price for supplies is minimal. For instance, I pay $0.14 for each Icy and sell them for $3 apiece. We're booked for multiple events now, which will spin off much more money.

The next venture was a medical vending business, purchased with a friend in September 2002, which also came from the CASHFLOW game that we were playing. The small machines sell aspirin and other emergency must-haves in restrooms. The deal card with the business struck a chord in us both. Excited over its possibilities, we saw that the machines served a need. Also, the business appealed to us because it was just a bit out of the norm.

We decided to meet with a business broker to determine what kind of vending machine opportunities were out there. Approaching several companies, we tried to obtain as much owner financing as possible while trying to acquire the best price on the machines.

Finally, we ended up going through a company we found online and bought twenty machines for $2,600. These machines were $160 less each than the ones the broker was offering. We were lucky in that a relative of my friend, who was supportive of our idea and wanted to help us, gave us $5,000. (It really is a gift. We don't have to repay it.) We are using the remaining $2,400 to pay for supplies.

The machines are being placed in exchange for charity. We hooked up with an organization called Child Quest International Services. This company finds missing children and provides us with sticker photos of the children to put on our machines in exchange for monthly donations. We informed the companies, whose products we stock, that we will be donating a portion of the proceeds to the organization. In turn, the companies can write off the two-by-two-foot space as a charitable contribution.

It took about sixty days to get the machines and then locate the items with which to fill the units. After we did that, our order was misplaced and it took a while to get every machine filled. However, now everything is running and the machines are in place. Through our research we discovered that each machine will bring in about $75 a month, and that's the low end. My friend and I will restock machines every two weeks. At present the machines are in a local area but who knows? Down the road we may expand. And as that happens we will hire people to stock the machines for us.

Prior to buying the businesses, we turned our home into an investment. In 2001 we rented out our house, which we bought in 1998 for $89,000. This 1,200 square foot single-family home with three bedrooms and two bathrooms brings us monthly passive income:

Cash put into property
Down payment:	$0
Closing costs paid by us:	$308
Repairs paid by us:	$0

Monthly cashflow analysis
Rental income:	$950
Monthly expenses:	
— Taxes (property) and insurance:	$124.84
— HOA (homeowners association) fee:	$10
— Loan payment (30 years at 7.375%):	$618.75
	$753.59
Net monthly cashflow:	$196.41

Cash-on-cash return

Annual cashflow ($196.41 × 12)	$2,356.92
÷	
Amount of cash put into property	308
Cash-on-cash return	765%

Comparable homes in the area are selling in a range from $110,000 to $119,000.

We do not use the money to pay off the house we live in. The fact is, we decided to rent the original house because the area it's in is fast rising in value. We wanted to keep the house. In the meantime, we figured we could get income out of it. Additionally, we were in the comfortable position of staying in the house until we rented it. That took all of sixty days, after which we stayed with friends until our new home was completed. Our first tenants signed a one-year lease and when it was up they left. The next month new tenants moved in and are still there. We have absolutely no regrets about doing this. It has been very easy and, thank heaven, our renters are great.

Lastly, we started running our promotions company, which was developed in 1996, in a different way because we changed our approach to it. In 2002, it made a gross profit of about $12,000. This is a significant contrast to the $1,000 the company earned yearly before we implemented Rich Dad lessons. For one thing, once I understood that the business was a vehicle to produce more income, my motivation to succeed rose. I didn't let the heckling by family members, friends, and even strangers bother me as I had let them do in the past. Most profoundly, I changed my perception of the business by telling myself three things:

1. There was nothing to be ashamed of.
2. I was doing something that the naysayers were not.
3. I was going to succeed. And you know, that's just what I'm doing!

A Different Perspective

Our lives have changed so much. I think in different ways now. In the past I defined risk as "how much will I lose?" Now I think of risk as "what do I need to do to educate myself in order to limit the amount of risk?"

I even created new habits by looking at financials differently. Writing down profits and losses, and seeing them on paper, gave us insight to what we were doing right or wrong. When I looked at them I felt a surge of excitement because I could see where we're going.

Then there's my team, which we put together to handle future ventures. It consists of a real estate broker, a tax attorney, an accountant, a marketing person, and a real estate investor. I trust what they, as a team, tell me. And while I admit that I don't quite feel super-successful enough to bring them together once a month, I know that eventually I will.

A More Secure Present, Too

After September 11, the resort industry took a big hit. A lot of people I knew were being laid off, and others, who held on to their jobs, weren't earning enough to make ends meet. Our situation was different. I knew that with what I had learned I would be okay. In 2002, when so many people were holding their breath, waiting for the other shoe to drop, I developed two businesses. When others felt afraid, I felt powerful. Self-determination gave me freedom from the fear of losing my job and freedom from worrying about the economy.

In my gut I always knew that someday we would be financially free. The problem was that I didn't know how to get there. Now I see where we're going and just knowing what is to come makes my day every day.

My co-workers, observing what I'm doing, see that they, too, can make choices that will change their lives. Then there are other people who say my husband and I are just lucky. They just don't get it!

The Future

My husband and I are still in the E (employee) and S (self-employed) cash-flow quadrants. I still work at the bar three days a week, which gets me lots of contacts, and David is a salesman for a beer distributor. Our aim is to switch our businesses—we don't employ anyone at present—into the B (business) and I (investment) quadrants along with our rental property.

In five years I'll be forty. When I reach that age I want to be in the position where I will never again have to work for someone else. To make that happen, I'm going to spend the next two years developing the businesses I currently own. At the same time I intend to educate myself in business development and real estate investing. At the end of this two-year phase I plan to leave my "day" job. The third and fourth years of my plan will be devoted to investing in real estate and educating myself about the stock market. Finally, the fifth and sixth years will be focused on setting up all we have in the business and investment quadrants so that cashflow will continue throughout our lives. Then I'll be able to give back a lot of what I've learned.

I intend to donate my time at my children's school. I want to teach the CASHFLOW for Kids game because it's so important for children to understand finance. This knowledge will give them the power to alter their lives.

My own kids (nine and ten years old) already know that money is out there for them to make. They're getting a financial education right now as they learn how important it is to save and to give.

Our lives truly changed, and continue to grow, because we took control of them. We never lost our dreams; we just found a way to make them come true.

Chapter 3

Never Too Late

CECILIA MORRISON
Scottsdale, Arizona

In the fall of 2002, I had the opportunity to speak to a sell-out crowd at Madison Square Garden in New York City with Robert Kiyosaki. Speaking in front of an audience of thousands of people isn't what I do normally; I'm a behind-the-scenes person at the Rich Dad organization.

I came to the Rich Dad office to fill a temporary two-week position. I had moved to Phoenix to retire after many years of working in the manufacturing sector in the Midwest.

During the past four years I worked in just about every job in the Rich Dad organization in a part-time capacity, including accounting and customer service. I am now the events coordinator who takes care of Robert's scheduling and as well as ordering merchandise for Rich Dad events. I put my retirement plans on hold.

I can usually be found with my notepad, referring to my list and taking notes: "Did the product arrive?" "Do they have the stage set up properly?"

To tell the truth, most of the time in the past I listened to what was going on out front but didn't really pay attention to it. That information, I figured, was for others, not for average people like my husband, George, and myself. In our late fifties, we're very independent people, so independent where money was concerned that we had no employer-supported pension and no retirement fund. As a self-employed part-time person I set my own hours and I don't receive any employee benefits.

If you took the most financially conservative person you could find and put her in that back room, that person would be me.

But that night a different person stood on the stage at Madison Square Garden. It's no small matter to change from a lifetime's view of money and take a step toward financial independence. But we did it, in a way we never would have considered if it were not for the Rich Dad information and the confidence I felt with my newfound knowledge.

Where I Come From

I grew up in Chicago, part of a strong blue-collar Catholic family. My parents were Polish immigrants; my father worked in the steel mills while my mother raised nine children. I'm the oldest. My family strove for a high school education for all of us. Where money was concerned I remember watching my grandmother save the old-fashioned way: She planted coffee cans filled with cash in the backyard.

I became an accountant, and worked for manufacturing companies. George became an independent contractor for a large computer company. We have two children. George and I made a lot of money and spent a lot of money. Still, we saved, like we were supposed to do. But we were always afraid to take money out of savings. We would earn income only as long as we got up Monday morning and went to work. We figured that we were comfortable. There was no need to go out there and shake the leaves.

But We're Shaken Up

Working at the Rich Dad office, I read the books and played CASHFLOW 101 with my colleagues. I finally began to get the drift that being so fiscally conservative was not the safest route to financial security. For a while I held fast to the notion that George and I could make changes "some other time, some other day."

Two years ago we bought a rental condo, right after attending a real estate seminar. But we went with the safe route and used cash on hand instead of other people's money (i.e., the bank's). Our cashflow was between $80 and $100 a month after expenses. It was a step but it certainly wasn't going to allow us to retire.

After attending another seminar where home equity loans were discussed, we realized that our home held a lot of investment potential. When we called a real estate agent to inspect our house to determine our equity, it turned out that the agent was a Robert Kiyosaki "junkie." We talked about real estate opportunities and ended up joining an LLC (limited liability company) with the real estate agent and eight other people. The idea was to leverage the $25,000 that each person was contributing in order to purchase a large real estate property (in the $1 million to $1.5 million range) that none of us could afford on our own.

For six months the properties brought to our attention were in a poor condition. We checked out each one. But we weren't comfortable with them because:

a) We didn't like the idea of being slumlords.

b) The return in cashflow was too slow. We didn't have time for cashflow to grow. We calculated that five to ten years was the maximum amount of time for people our age to have an investment return passive income to live on. There was another factor to consider: We would be tying up between $25,000 and $75,000. We realized that our children could benefit from it in the future. But our aim was to have it benefit us for our retirement now.

(The investment group is no longer together. However, we keep in touch, as we are always open to a once-in-a-lifetime offer. We met our accountant through the group and we have gained a valuable advisor.)

Still, our goal was to invest $50,000 to gain an immediate return. I remembered that one of the deal cards in the CASHFLOW game mentioned laundromats. We knew for sure that neither of us wanted to quit our positions to run a business full-time, and we realized that a laundromat could give us that freedom.

First we checked franchises on-line and then drove around to look at local possibilities. We called three major brokers in town through the Coin Laundry Association and told them what we were looking for. The process took eight months but we learned a lot during that time. We finally lucked out by finding one in good condition where the owners were going through a divorce.

Without touching our savings, we were able to use equity in our home to buy the business, all without an impact to our lifestyle. To protect us against liability, we set up a separate corporation. We've learned to keep our eyes on the utility bills—water, electricity, and gas—since the utilities are the greatest expenses.

We were able to assume the former owners' SBA (Small Business Association) loan, which required a high down payment but gave us a five-year loan. On this schedule we will own the equipment free and clear in five years, which is important to us because that is when we plan to fully retire. Since our purchase price was for equipment only we can deduct the tax depreciation on the equipment as well as the other business expenses, which gives us virtually nontaxable monthly cashflow.

We will recoup our investment fully in the next five years. With a yearly income of $95,000 and expenses of $56,000, we are receiving a cash return of $39,000 annually. This will increase as our equipment loan is paid in full. Our yearly income will reach $60,000 at that time.

This investment is paying off so well we've set up an equity line of credit at a mortgage broker so that we can buy two more laundromats, our goal by the end of two years. Five years from now we can maintain our lifestyle and not work unless we choose to.

For now George wants to stop traveling so much. He has left every Monday and returned on Friday for twenty-five years. While he doesn't want to retire yet, he does want to be more in control of which jobs he takes. We're still in our home, which we love, but we've made some changes. For instance, we traded an expensive car in for a smaller SUV, which is used for the laundromat supplies, and saved $300 a month.

Our Children React

Our son, who is twenty-seven, became interested in what we are doing. He took CASHFLOW 101 to his dormitory when he was in college and has already talked to a real estate agent about buying rental property.

Our daughter is twenty-three and, having observed what we are doing, asked her brother for the CASHFLOW game to play. She and her brother are talking about going into a real estate investment together.

For George and me, the situation is different. With our background, and at our age, it's hard to do catch-up because doing so requires changing long-established habits and points of view. We were skeptical about change: "Show it to us" was our attitude. We felt that Social Security would be waiting for us, but seeing our parents' struggle while trying to live on it was a big eye-opener. Sure, compared to our parents we were doing great. We thought we were doing the right thing by saving. Unfortunately, we lost six figures in the stock market the last two years. This was blood-and-sweat money that was earned with hard work.

Truthfully, when I wrote the check for the laundromat my hand shook. But having written the first one, every one that follows will be easier. And knowing that we won't have to depend on either our children or on Social Security gives us a great feeling of security. In just a few years, when George reaches sixty, we'll be set up. Being in control feels really good. I've worked hard for other people and companies and helped them make money all my life—but this money is mine. In fact, I've just sponsored a local Little League team (one of George's and my passions). It feels so great to give back to the community. I love to see the name of our laundromat on the kids' shirts and on a banner on the field.

If you are in your fifties, or older, and think you can't change your attitude about finances and opportunities, believe me, you can. Once I understood from Rich Dad that we could really buy a business that would give us monthly cashflow to support us, I was ready to walk out on that stage and tell that to the arena full of people in Madison Square Garden that if I could do it, so could they.

Part II

Where You've Been, Where You Can Go

My rich dad showed me that it was possible to change the way I felt about money.

I know that money is a very emotional subject. People feel excited or scared or a lot of other emotions when they have to cope with money. So I am not surprised when people tell me how their Rich Dad experiences tapped into their emotional states. How their families either dealt with, or ignored, money matters influenced their feelings. Fears about mismanaging money, having too much of it and alienating others, or looking incompetent, were real problems.

Overcoming conflicted feelings about money is often hard to do. Using the Rich Dad resources, these people changed their feelings about money, and therefore themselves, because they learned to take control of their money. Instead of allowing money to rule them, they took charge of their money. No matter what their backgrounds were, they were able to achieve financial freedom.

Meet David Lukas. A resident of Arkansas, he is honest about his lack of confidence about money. But that didn't stop him once he realized what he was capable of doing with the right help. Becoming financially educated made all the difference for David, whose story is a source of inspiration for any person who has ever felt that he or she couldn't succeed at anything, much less securing assets for financial security.

Across the country in Washington State, Valerie Collymore, M.D., has another story to tell. Both my poor dad and my rich dad talked a lot about education, and how important it was for boys and girls to go to school in order to learn a profession or skill. Contributing to society was necessary. But students didn't receive a financial education because the schools didn't teach it. And that left a lot people in precarious financial situations. That's what happened to Valerie.

Highly educated in medicine, she nonetheless admits that managing money was something she avoided because she was afraid of making mistakes. Her Rich Dad journey takes her from fearing money to taking control of it. Planning a secure financial future for herself and her family is her goal and she is focused and determined to achieve it.

Reed Schweizer, in Indiana, offers his story. Admitting that he didn't understand money, he experienced a number of financial ups and downs until he found Rich Dad's guidance. After reading the Rich Dad materials he started seeing opportunities that he was never aware of before and he began acquiring assets to build his future.

And you'll meet Dan McKenzie, who lives in North Carolina. We share a strong emotional childhood memory. His father and my poor dad both felt that money was the basis for all that was wrong in the world. In reading Rich Dad, Dan was reassured that his feelings about money weren't wrong and that acquiring assets was right. If you were brought up with the idea that evil and cash were connected and therefore you should avoid money, read Dan's story. He reveals the real significance of financial freedom, all the good it can do, and the importance of giving back.

Chapter 4

Building Confidence One Property at a Time

DAVID LUKAS
Little Rock, Arkansas

While I was growing up in Jacksonville, Arkansas, all the way through high school, I had little confidence in my abilities to succeed at anything. Because I didn't do well as a student in traditional education classes, I wasn't motivated enough to even try to succeed.

Yet, two years ago, when I was twenty-five years old and without money, I found the motivation to begin my financial education after a friend in a network marketing company handed me a tape. As I listened to it in my car, Robert Kiyosaki sparked my attention. I felt that he was talking to me. What he said made such sense. *Buy assets. Lessen liabilities.* These were attainable goals. I could do them. I wanted to learn how. I had always been interested in real estate and now I was beginning to see that investing in properties was the way to build a strong financial future.

I spent a couple of months reading as many books as possible on real estate investing and listening to more tapes. Little by little I could not only see where I wanted to go—my aim was to invest in real estate—but also how to get there. Inspiration to take action was taking hold. I could see how to put the puzzle pieces in place.

Supported by a newly discovered determination and ongoing lessons in my financial education, I realized that my desire to succeed was greater than either my fear of failure or my fear of the unknown. Finally I came to understand that doing nothing would always result in zero success. Doing something meant overcoming my fears and channeling them into ways to find financial freedom.

In the last year and a half, I've invested roughly $185,000 of my banker's money into rental property, which is cumulatively appraised at $225,000. I own two two-bedroom duplexes and one three-bedroom duplex along with a three-bedroom home and a one-bedroom apartment for a total of eight rental units. While my investment was minimal—*$2,000 to purchase all the properties*—my monthly cashflow is about $1,500.

As amazing as it sounds, the journey from being afraid to try to embracing success has been very fast. I never dreamed that I could achieve so much in so little time. But the reality is that I did—and continue to do so.

My First Business Experience

After a year of college, in 1996 I dropped out and co-founded an Internet service provider that specialized in filtering out unwanted Web sites for families and businesses.

I thought of myself as being self-employed. From 1999 to 2001 I ran the business, along with five employees, from an office building in Sherwood, Arkansas, a town about eight miles outside Little Rock. By this time my co-founder had left. I was accountable to the shareholders, the twenty-five local investors who had given us start-up money. These people saw potential in the business plan and made it possible for the service to begin. At one point, we had approximately 1,000 customers.

However, after five years, the investors decided that they no longer wanted to put in any money and the service was sold. I lost my $5,000 investment and ultimately the venture was not profitable.

Then, in 2001, I founded an Internet-based long-distance provider that offered service in the United States and Canada. The subscriber base was sold after a short time.

But despite the short run of both of these businesses, I regard them as the best on-the-front-line business education I could ever get. After all, I was barely out of high school when the first business began. I wouldn't trade the real-world education that I gained in starting and running businesses for anything. I acquired valuable skills in dealing with the public, picking up the phone and calling strangers, marketing, billing, outsourcing, raising capital, sales, operations, and problem solving. Sure, I made a lot of mistakes, but I learned from every one of them. This experience was a terrific foundation on which to build my future real estate business.

It was time to start. Leah, my wife, supported us for a year and a half while I began to acquire properties.

Here's How I Did It

The search for properties began by my looking in the newspaper and in real estate magazines. I drove around different neighborhoods and talked with people in my local landlord association.

I knew what I wanted in regard to monthly cashflow, so I used forms to figure the potential cashflow of a particular property.

After this I just went out and made an offer. To my surprise the first offer I made was accepted. Let me stop right here and tell you: I didn't expect this to happen. If I had to make ten offers on properties I would have. The point is that I was committed to buying real estate and I was determined to give this objective all the time and attention it required.

Then, of course, I needed a mortgage. I explained to the first bank I went to that the current owner of the property was going to carry a second note. In reply I was told that I was required to put at least 10 percent of my own money down. This didn't work for me because I didn't have any money. But I did have the option to go to another bank, which is just what I did.

The second bank was not as particular and did not care if the down payment was borrowed. Consequently, this is the bank I've used for all of my real estate investment purchases.

My second investment property was also purchased with no money down. The seller of the property loaned me the down payment that the bank required. The owner carried a 10 percent second note on this one.

(One of the most significant plusses was that I negotiated for these sellers to carry a second note on these properties. This worked in my favor because I started out with no money to invest. I would not have been able to acquire the property if the sellers had not agreed to do so. Both of these notes are for less than four years. So in a few years my cashflow will increase because I will have paid off some of the owner-financed second mortgages.)

On the third property purchase, I convinced my parents to loan me the money from the line of credit secured by their home. I purchased a three-bedroom home as well as a one-bedroom apartment for $35,000. I spent about $2,000 on the two purchases and I did almost all of the repair work myself. Otherwise, I would not have been able to afford the improvements to the property. A few months later I went to the bank and informed them that since I owned these properties free and clear, I wanted to get a loan secured by them.

The two properties were appraised for $50,000 and the bank loaned me 90 percent of the appraisal amount, which was around $45,000. After paying closing costs, loan fees, and repaying my parents, I pocketed $8,800.

Here's the breakdown:

Purchase price: $35,000

Cash put into property

Down payment:	$500
Closing costs paid by me:	$0
Repairs/renovations paid by me:	$2,000
	$2,500

Monthly cashflow analysis

Rental income:	$1,010
— Vacancy loss (5%):	$50.50
Total income:	$959.50

Monthly expenses:
(Note: The tenants are responsible for all utilities and yard work.)

— Taxes (property) and insurance:	$75
— Repairs/maintenance:	$0
— Reserve:	$25
— Management fee:	$0
— Loan payment (15 years at 7.4%):	$423
	$523

(Note: The bank has an accelerated payment plan that allows me to pay $423 bimonthly. Doing this should pay off the first mortgage in around thirteen years.)

Net monthly cashflow:	$436.50

Cash-on-cash return
Annual cashflow ($436.50 × 12)	$5,238
÷	
Amount of cash put into property	$2,500
Cash-on-cash return	209%

Today the house is appraised at $50,000.

My fourth property was purchased like my third. I borrowed the money from my parents and paid cash for the property. Without any repairs or improvements, the property was appraised for $75,000 ($15,000 more than I paid for it). I went to my bank and once again told them that I owned this property free and clear and my goal was to obtain a loan with the property as collateral. The bank loaned me enough to pay back the loan from my parents, as well as all closing costs and loan fees. While I did not have any extra cash left from this transaction, I've done quite well. Here's the breakdown for the three-bedroom duplex:

Purchase price: $60,000

Cash put into property
Down payment:	$500
Closing costs paid by me:	$0
Repairs/renovations paid by me:	$2,500
	$3,000

Monthly cashflow analysis
Rental income:	$1,300
– Vacancy loss (5%):	$65
Total income:	$1,235

Monthly expenses:
(Note: The tenants are responsible for all utilities and yard work.)

– Taxes (property) and insurance:	$80
– Repairs/maintenance:	$0
– Reserve:	$35
– Management fee:	$0
– Loan payment (15 years at 6.5%):	$622.66
	$737.66
Net monthly cashflow:	$497.34

Cash-on-cash return

Annual cashflow ($497.34 × 12)	$5,968.08
÷	
Amount of cash put into property	$3,000
Cash-on-cash return	198%

Today the house is appraised at $75,000.

Here's the breakdown on a two-bedroom duplex. The seller carried a second mortgage in the amount of $4,550 for 36 months.

Purchase price: $43,000

Cash put into property

Down payment:	$500
Closing costs paid by me:	$0
Repairs/renovations paid by me:	$600
	$1,100

Monthly cashflow analysis

Rental income:	$1,000
– Vacancy loss (5%):	$50
Total income:	$950

Monthly expenses:
(Note: The tenants are responsible for all utilities and yard work.)

–Taxes (property) and insurance:	$75
–Repairs/maintenance:	$ 0
–Management fee:	$ 0
–Reserve:	$25
–Loan payment (15 years at 7.4%):	$405.28

(Note: The bank has an accelerated payment plan that allows me to pay $405.28 bimonthly. Doing this should pay the first mortgage off in about thirteen years.)

–Second mortgage paid to seller (36 months at 8.0%):	$148.50
	$653.78
Net monthly cashflow:	$296.22

Cash-on-cash return

Annual cashflow ($296.22 × 12)	$3,554.64
÷	
Cash put into property	$1,100
Cash-on-cash return	323%

Today the house is appraised at $50,000.

Right now I remain a small deal investor. Each property I've bought has been priced between $35,000 and $60,000. But I must be honest. Like any business real estate can cause headaches. Pipes can burst. Units can remain vacant longer than you'd prefer. But these are temporary setbacks. Once the determination to succeed takes over, the rewards of investing far outweigh the need for the occasional aspirin. I still cannot believe the return on investment I've seen relative to the actual dollar amounts I've spent. Perseverance pays.

From August 2001 to December 2002 I was self-employed. I founded a corporation for the purpose of investing in real estate. However, right now, in addition to acquiring real estate, I'm concentrating on paying off some liabilities like car payments and credit card debt. To do that I actually went out and found a day job. Also, recently my wife, Leah's, income has dropped drastically due to the uncertain economy. She earns a straight commission doing wholesale distribution on general merchandise.

In one to two years I plan on eliminating our major liability payments (excluding our home). At the same time we'll be building up our passive income.

Where I Go from Here

My immediate goals are to continue leveraging my earned income by using my bank's money to buy more residential real estate. By 2006 my objective is to own sixteen rental properties or units. By 2010 I will own a minimum of forty rental units, generating cashflow of $10,000 a month or more.

By the time I'm forty I will have paid off the mortgages on no fewer than ten properties. Then I intend to sell them, as well as others I will acquire, and transfer the money into an IRS-approved 1031 exchange. I'll use the proceeds as a down payment on a larger piece of property. Say I sell the ten properties for $60,000 each. That $600,000 will provide the down payment on a large apartment complex. The IRS gives property owners who do this a break and defers the capital gains tax when the properties are sold.

By this time my monthly cashflow should be between $18,000 and $20,000 a month.

The Future Is Bright

Money is important; there's no denying it. But there are other factors in life that count for even more. My dad, a pharmacist, is self-employed and always worked long hours. People needed his expertise and services and he didn't disappoint them. However, he couldn't be in two places at once; if he was at his job, he couldn't be at home. I don't want that to happen to me. (Although I'm delighted to report that my parents—my father is close to retirement—as well as my aunt and uncle have been buying investment properties in the last two and a half years.)

I'm twenty-seven years old. There are no words to describe how good it feels to be in control of my financial destiny. At the same time it's so exciting to know that my income will not be dependent on someone other than myself. If there's any bigger confidence builder than that, I surely don't know what it is.

Chapter 5

A Different Education

VALERIE L. COLLYMORE, M.D.
Bellevue, Washington

About three years ago I arrived at a financial crossroads. I could see two choices up ahead. I could continue to creep along the slow-moving economic side road that I had traveled my entire life. I kept to this one-lane route because my fear of appearing financially stupid outweighed my desire to become financially smart. My second choice was to accelerate onto the financial freeway filled with fast-moving cars steered by financially savvy and wealthy people who knew how to get where they wanted to go.

The financial superhighway beckoned but I was stuck on the onramp. I needed more than a push. A new fuel source and a different map that would reveal routes to the world I longed to inhabit were essential.

An interesting occurrence pushed me to that crossroads. My family and I were living in Denver, where I had become involved in the world of charitable giving. Through volunteering, I met a couple of people who were refreshingly up-front about their modest educational backgrounds. They did not see themselves as being particularly intellectually gifted. They were, however, very wealthy.

I learned, by watching and listening to these individuals, that there was another form of "smart" that went beyond advanced degrees. I'll admit that finding this out shook me up. I realized that there were other lessons to be learned that didn't rely on what I knew so well: grades and degrees and diplomas that were supposed to insure a financially secure existence. An intense desire for a completely different way to live, one that was not dependent on salaries, took hold. I began to see a way to achieve the goal of having time to enjoy family, serve my community, and pursue personal interests, while simultaneously securing our financial future.

I started to believe that I, too, could achieve the peace of mind that goes with financial confidence. I wanted to find a way to educate myself to be clever in a whole new way. As I opened my mind to this possibility, I began to seek the information I required. I remember thinking that a teacher appears when a person is ready to learn.

Soon after, during one of my frequent scavenges at a local bookstore, I found *Rich Dad Poor Dad*. As I read it, several emotions hit me one after another. First, pain kicked in, as I was forced to confront all of the dim-witted behaviors I relied on. Then I experienced relief, quickly followed by excitement. I realized that the book was not only showing me how to dig myself out of the financial mess that I had created. It was also showing me how to achieve my financial dreams, essentially by acquiring new ways of thinking and behaving. I understood that the lessons were meant to be used by each person in a unique way. For me, that meant applying the information for the benefit of my husband, my daughters, my mother, and my future grandchildren, as a first step. Then, in the future, I could take the lessons and use them as a tool for giving to others, a feeling that filled me with joy.

While reading the book, I found the guts to dare to reach for something better, both financially and emotionally.

A Great Education Only Goes So Far

My predicament might sound odd when I tell you that I'm a doctor; pediatric medicine is my area of expertise. Furthermore, I am married to a physician who specializes in internal medicine. We met the first week of medical school, at Columbia University's College of Physicians and Surgeons in New York City. Education was always regarded as a very high priority in my family. My father's parents had earned graduate school degrees, an accomplishment relatively unusual for African-Americans at that time. My husband and

I, who are in our forties, continually stressed the importance of a good education to our two teenage daughters.

But despite the academic accomplishments, the health and good fortune of our children, the good incomes (relative to what our parents earned), the rewarding community interactions, and the bright prospects, I knew a crucial piece was missing. That piece was a sense of long-term financial security.

My husband, my daughters, and I lived comfortably. We spent some of our income on decent homes, travel, and nice cars. We made the maximum contributions each year to our 401(k). But I often purchased more doodads than either my children or I needed. All looked good on the surface, but more often than I care to admit, we spent foolish amounts for no other good reason than to please others, to behave as doctors were expected to behave.

The way we structured our lives led to another problem. Acutely aware of the burnout suffered by physicians and of the less than secure corporate climate of the past few years, I began to dare to ask myself that very scary question: What would happen if my husband wanted or had to leave his profession? We were entirely dependent on his income.

Nine years ago I took a leave from a very rewarding but highly demanding and stressful position as an attending physician at the Children's Hospital of Los Angeles, where I practiced pediatric emergency trauma medicine. Putting my family first, I focused on raising our daughters and caring for my terminally ill mother-in-law.

Despite my advanced education, I maintained an astonishing degree of financial ignorance. I worried about my routine of frequently getting into salvageable amounts of debt and I fretted about our financial future. I did not apply, in my financial affairs, the exquisite discipline and logic that brought success in the medical field. I did not obsessively avoid mistakes as I did in my medical practice, but often repeated dumb financial behaviors.

Added to all of this discomfort was the guilty realization that I was not eager to return to work in the emergency trauma field. I worried and worried but had no clear plan of action until I read *Rich Dad Poor Dad*. With a surge of gratitude and relief, I began using ideas discussed in this book to craft a plan of action. The more I read and learned, the more passion I felt toward acquiring a financial education. A strong passion very similar to the one that propelled me into medicine began to take hold. Here also was a vehicle for changing lives.

Shifting lifestyles have been a constant theme in my life, but in the past the lifestyle change was imposed *on* me. I was not yet the one taking the financial reins and *making* the change happen.

Mother Makes Invention Necessary

When I was two years old and my brother, David, was four, our father, who was a doctor, died. My mother earned a living as a nurse and for seven more years we remained in Camden, New Jersey, where I was born.

By the time I was nine, my mother decided she had had enough of cold winters and the even colder shoulders of peers who did not seem displeased by our diminished lifestyle. She decided that we should travel to the French Riviera, which sounded very exotic to me. I thought we would spend the summer there and then I would return to the fourth grade and my Brownie troop. I ended up staying there until I was eighteen, and ready for college.

Certainly there were many wonderful aspects to living in Nice, France. The academic and music education and the athletic training (track was my favored sport) were excellent and free. I learned to speak fluent French and studied Russian, German, and a bit of Arabic. The landscape was spectacular, the culture enriching, and the beaches unforgettable.

While living on Social Security and VA benefits (my father had been a veteran), we managed to fit our rather impoverished selves into the social strata of the Riviera. During the summers we traveled around Europe, living in a tent pitched on various camping grounds. We discovered more by impulsive wandering than by careful planning. More than once, we attended very glitzy performances of world-renowned ballet artists such as Rudolf Nureyev and Margot Fonteyn. At the end of those memorable evenings, we would retire to our tent.

Although this rather unusual lifestyle, with its travel and proximity to famed artists and glamour, was highly prized by my adventurous and intrepid mother, our financial situation was precarious, living as we did from small check to small check. Divine guidance, sheer bravado, and luck were frequently relied on. The dull and disciplined pursuit of long-range planning did not seem to fit with the fun of this rather impulsive and "carefree" lifestyle.

At the start of the summer when I was twelve, my mother decided to decamp to Greece for the season and arranged with the American consulate to retrieve and forward our next check to the small village on the sea in Italy where we would be stopping along the way. The first day no check appeared. Nor did it show up on the second day, or the third. By the end of day two the last of our money had been spent on dinner, so by day three, without breakfast or lunch, my brother and I were feeling hungry. We were also bored, and out of that boredom and necessity grew a business.

My very artistic brother, then fourteen years old, started making a cement paste from mashed algae and stone dust as I began collecting and pulverizing colored stones. Together we fashioned, on large flat stones, renditions of the blue sea, the rocky beaches, and the green islands offshore. Pleased with our efforts, we branched out into pictures of animals and marine life, although I must confess that my brother displayed a gift for art that far surpassed mine. (Years later he graduated from the Harvard School of Design.)

By the time the after-dinner crowd of tourists strolled by we had quite a collection. Then one person asked how much a stone cost. Thus was born a small business successful enough to feed the three of us at the local restaurant for the next two days until the check arrived.

A seed was planted: If you need income, be true to yourself and follow your instincts.

Another seed took root as well. Our home base on the Riviera was chock-full of retired CEOs. As we got to know some of them I observed that they lived well, if not extravagantly. I never heard these individuals discuss money. And I never acknowledged or discussed the significant economic gap between them and us. I took great pride in the fact that, though I did not have money, I had other qualities to offer, including the ability and desire to work hard. I cultivated and deepened these and other qualities.

It seemed to me that talking about money was not a classy thing to do. So I never did. Yet I did not stop yearning for a knowledgeable financial mentor who would somehow discover my hidden interest in financial security and find me worthy to take on as their student. I spent years hoping for a mentor who would lift the curtain and reveal the secrets of the financially secure and who would dispute the negative, limiting views of money that I heard over and over again when I was growing up:

"It takes money to make money."

"No matter how hard you try you just can't get ahead."

"We might as well enjoy life now and spend the little money we have."

"If you're a good person you'll be provided for."

"The rich get richer."

I remember thinking, "How do you get on that 'rich getting richer' path?"

It took an earthquake to wake me out of this dream and start up taking control of my financial life.

Ignorance Is Never Bliss

By 1994, my husband, daughters, and I were living in California. Two weeks before the Northridge earthquake hit, our insurance agent visited our house to collect signatures for renewing our homeowners policy and specifically to advise my husband against his earlier decision to decline the renewal of our $400 per year earthquake policy. Since my husband was detained, he called to urge me to sign the papers.

When the agent arrived we sat down and I heard her speaking but I was so afraid of appearing stupid that I just nodded my head and smiled and zoned out. I didn't ask one question. I just signed the document.

After that terrible and destructive earthquake, first we made sure that family and neighbors were safe and then we handled the minor injuries that a couple of neighbors sustained. I recall being deeply unsettled by the pallor of my husband's face when many of the neighbors, assembled in the dark cul-de-sac that memorable night, were thanking their lucky stars that they had great earthquake insurance coverage.

I was able to reach our insurance agent the next morning and asked that a copy of the waiver be faxed to us. When the page came through I was shocked to see my signature under the clause that canceled the earthquake policy.

Our earthquake damage was assessed at $47,000. We had about $45,000 in cash savings. That was the last document I ever signed without paying attention to everything that was in it.

It took an earthquake and nearly $50,000 in repair bills for me to realize that my ignorance of money matters could result in acute financial distress. I also realized that there is financial wisdom in the saying that "two heads are better than one." For about a year I chided myself about my idiotic action and finally accepted that I had to move forward. Wanting the responsibility, I oversaw the rebuilding of our home. This was a pivotal period for me; I began to flex barely used muscles. I interviewed contractors. I listened and asked questions. I spoke up and said no when required. I read contracts until I understood them.

I found I could overcome the "'brain freeze'" that often plagued me in business situations by "daring to seem dumb" by asking every little question, sometimes repeatedly, until I had a very clear picture. By looking upon the agent or contractor as my "employee" paid by me to teach and inform me at my leisure and discretion, I could put the fear of failing or being out of my depth on the back burner and get on with the business at hand.

This period turned out to be a preparatory course for finding *Rich Dad Poor Dad*.

Financial Independence 101

By the time I read *Rich Dad Poor Dad*, I was ready to take on the responsibility for rebuilding our financial future. Early in our marriage I was only too happy to hand over financial responsibilities to my husband because I wanted to believe that he could carry the entire load on his shoulders. He would check off various boxes next to investment options in his 401(k) plan and I would glow, feeling so safe and so proud of my man, while remaining completely clueless about the subject matter at hand. I chose not to know. I thrived on being taken care of and was comfortable focusing on the spending part of this deal. I am not a lazy person by any means. Many of my peers think of me as a workaholic. But in hindsight, I was mentally lazy about finances. And I was fearful of rocking the boat.

As my husband's career became more complex and demanding, with increasing business travel and less free time, it became difficult for us to allocate the time needed to handle our now expanding financial needs. Stress has a very interesting way of bringing out maladaptive behaviors and illogical thinking. Overspending was simply easier, in the short run, than acquiring the knowledge and the discipline to achieve a balance sheet that would show positive monthly cashflow.

Devoid of my own financial skills yet realizing that something needed to be done, I placed additional burdens at the feet of my already overburdened husband. Weren't the finances *his* chore? If mistakes were made, wasn't this *his* fault? If I overspent, wasn't *he* supposed to teach me how not to overspend? After the spectacular failure of this line of thinking, I realized that I had come dangerously close to being a complete sucker when it came to money management. Someone with the time and the passion—namely me—had to take control of our finances.

For instance, we had turned over the responsibility of making decisions regarding stocks to a financial planner. He turned out to be a commission-receiving broker who peddled the same ten tech-heavy securities to all his clients. Despite asking many of the right questions during the initial interview, I didn't fully understand or investigate his answers because, once more, I did not want to appear unintelligent or underconfident, especially since my husband, who reluctantly but dutifully gave in to my wishes to hire this planner, was present. I did, however, inform the broker that I would be following his picks and that I would gradually take on more of the decision-making process as my financial education progressed.

When I began tracking several test stocks on a daily basis, reading the prospectus of each one, as well as tracking them in business papers and journals, I became alarmed. One stock was Lucent. Another was Nortel. Another was JDS Uniphase. Then there was Corning. Even to my inexperienced eyes, the idea of holding rapidly declining stocks in the face of what seemed to be an increasingly likely economic meltdown seemed downright reckless. I began to ask my broker and his associates many questions.

I also began to break the "don't talk about money" taboo by sharing my thoughts and ideas with a couple of highly successful businesspersons, a technique that I now frequently use. I say to them, "Here are my thoughts and my analysis. Is this how you see it?"

When the broker returned fewer and fewer of my calls, I took action. Thanks to the education I was gaining from Rich Dad, I realized that the notion of independent thinking was more than just okay. It was a necessity. I researched financial planners for the correct credentials, interviewed them, and checked up on my choices on government Web sites. I decided what the financial allocations would be prior to the first meeting with the new financial advisor. I did it for two reasons. One, I wanted to establish that I was an independent thinker capable of making rational decisions. Two, I was afraid he would try to talk us out of those decisions!

We switched our entire portfolio to a new and nationally recognized planner who earned the highest credentials in the financial planning field. Though we eventually suffered, like so many others, a loss (approximately 25 percent of our portfolio), we were spared a major disaster because we sold virtually all of the former stock fund picks. But something even more far-reaching happened.

To overcome my fear of making a mistake, given my vast lack of knowledge where the stock market was concerned, I researched and selected two test stocks that made sense to me and I tracked them. Then I bought a number of shares to up the ante of my commitment level. One is doing quite well and the other has all the earmarks of a well-run, financially sound stock although its price has dropped. This terrific experience taught me the value of being informed. Control meant deciding what the financial planner would handle, and what I would deal with myself.

At home, another profound change was taking place. On more than one occasion I had run up bad credit card debt due to uncontrolled spending, which I justified with rather silly psychobabble and excuses ("I deserve it." "I left my medical career for my family." "I'm married to a doctor."). I'm happy to say that these "reasons," and others like them, are now retired.

We were extremely fortunate in that our income has allowed us to get out of that debt on more than one occasion. However, I began to see that each dollar wasted on paying for bad debt was a lost opportunity for that money to grow. Finally facing my problem without flinching, I set realistic financial goals, confronted the many changes within our household that would need to take place in order to succeed in this endeavor, and knuckled down to learn more about money management and accounting. I plan to *never* fall into that overspending syndrome again.

Inspired by Rich Dad, I created my own little balance sheets that included income and expenses. These monthly sheets not only showed me what a mess I had made of things; they also helped me to focus efforts on optimizing the numbers. It was almost like a game; would we come out ahead *this* month? I won't soon forget the day when assets dwarfed liabilities according to Rich Dad accounting, thanks to a small windfall and our decision to use it wisely. We saw the asset column grow while the liability column shrank considerably. At last, I could track our money. I was ready to invest in real estate.

Here's How I Did It

First of all, I determined what kind of down payment we could afford; about $20,000 was right for us the first time around. If this amount was 20 percent of the price of a home, then we could afford a home that cost about $100,000. We were lucky to find an area in which we could find single-family homes for this price and even luckier that these were located in good school districts, in fairly nice neighborhoods and near an army base, which insured consistent and reliable renters. In contrast, I do not feel comfortable with studios, which I associate with a more transient population. I wanted a win-win situation, where the renter wins because he can afford a nice home in a decent neighborhood in a good school district at a fair price. With these factors in place he is likely to be a long-term and contented tenant. Then we would win, too, because the rent will be paid on time, cashflow will be consistent, and in fifteen years optimally, the mortgage will be paid off, ensuring greater cashflow. We found a two-bedroom, two-bathroom home that met our criteria.

I had the financing fully in place before seriously looking for a property. I asked the lender to provide a letter stating what we could afford to pay and what the bank was willing to lend us. Also, our credit rating is excellent, so our real estate agent can honestly tell a seller that they will experience no problems with us as buyers. We discussed with the agent ahead of time specific purchase prices and lower limits and upper limits, and then gave him a free hand. Everything was decided before negotiations started. I also made sure that my spouse was fully on board; due to his earned income, lenders want him involved.

Needing an $82,000 mortgage, I asked the lender to calculate the monthly payments on a fifteen-year loan at 7.25 percent interest (this was in the early spring of 2002). This came to $755.85. We asked the property manager/agent what he was sure he could rent the home for. His answer was $800 in its current state with an increase of $30 to $35 after one year. However, I forgot about his fee of 7 percent when making the calculations. Not only did I not originally factor in the fee, I didn't factor in taxes or insurance either. Here are my calculations on the house that we purchased for $103,500 *before* I corrected my error:

Cash put into property

Down payment:	$22,930
Closing costs paid by us:	$2,676
Repairs/renovations paid by us:	$0
	$25,606

Monthly cashflow analysis

Rental income:	$800
Monthly expenses:	
— Management fee:	$56
— Loan payment (15 years at 7.25%):	$755.85
	$811.85
Net monthly cashflow:	($11.25)

But as pleased as we were to own this house, something was wrong. Not only was the cashflow negative, there were other costs, like taxes and insurance, that the rental fee was not covering. This property was not self-sustaining.

Now I saw the *real* picture. I had planned to use proceeds from the property that we own free and clear to pay the property tax and insurance and any future repairs on the newly acquired property. This was "fuzzy" accounting indeed! You see, twelve years ago we bought a single-family residence for investment purposes in Southern California for $101,000. Several weeks ago it was valued at $156,000. The annual expenses total $2,100 and the net rent is $963. I figured this home could pay the bills on the new home. This was wrong.

Getting more numbers together, I realized that refinancing the property with a thirty-year mortgage (I was in a hurry to own it free and clear in fifteen years) would produce positive cashflow. The mortgage payments would drop to the low $500s from the present $755. There would be enough funds to pay taxes and insurance (property taxes were about $1,298 a year, the homeowners insurance was $309, and the earthquake insurance came to $252). Any small positive cashflow would be left to accumulate for repairs and act as a reserve fund. Here are the revised numbers and, in the far right column, the numbers for a rent increase to $850, effective in May 2003:

Monthly cashflow analysis

Rental income:		$800	$850
Monthly expenses:			
— Taxes (property):	$108.17		
— Property insurance:	$25.75		
— Earthquake insurance:	$21		
— Maintenance:	$0		
— Reserve for repairs:	$45		
— Management fee (7% of rent):		$56	$59.50
— Loan payment (30 years at 6.5%):	$520		
		$775.92	$779.42
Net monthly cashflow:		$24.08	$70.58

Cash-on-cash return (present)

Annual cashflow ($24 × 12)	$288
÷	
Amount of cash put into property	$25,606
Cash-on-cash return	1.1%

Cash-on-cash return (future)

Annual cashflow ($70.58 × 12)	$846.96
÷	
Amount of cash put into property	$25,606
Cash-on-cash return	3.3%

Despite my error, I was very excited when this belated "light bulb" finally turned on. There is no experience that can substitute for actually going through a deal and making a few mistakes along the way. Even better, I figured out what was wrong and I knew how to fix it. At first, I just wanted to buy a property close to the other property that we owned, not get ripped off, and pay it off in fifteen years. After reading and absorbing more of the various Rich Dad books, my goal changed to making the numbers on that property look better, i.e., positive cashflow and better cash-on-cash return. In time I will extract funds from a future refinance to use toward the down payment on another property.

I plan to move forward with additional purchases. I have set, as a first step, the goal of owning ten properties. Within fifteen to eighteen years the positive cashflow from the properties will add significantly to our retirement income.

A Team Effort

The first time around is really time-consuming and demanding and somewhat intimidating. Having mentors or advisors or even like-minded individuals to talk to during this process is *crucial*. I am lucky to have recognized the need for this kind of support and to have had the good fortune of being selected as a participant for the Rich Dad coaching program.

When faced with the actual real-life details and obstacles and problems of real estate investing, it is a huge advantage to be able to call on knowledgeable people. The questions I ask include, "What would you do?" "What have you done when you were faced with this situation?" "What do I need to know?" "What mistake did you make?" and "How can I get around this obstacle?"

My team includes:

• An excellent and much published lawyer who is handling a new estate plan because we're now living in a community property state. Our attorney is also handling placement of property into LLCs (limited liability companies).

• A private banking group, which offered a substantial line of credit and private banking services.

• An expanding list of real estate contacts in a few states (agents and brokers).

• An accountant and a few knowledgeable contacts within the franchise tax board and board of equalization of the state in which we own property.

• A short list of mentors. These days I cringe a lot less when the mentor responds with, "Actually, my view is the exact opposite of what you suggest." I continue to learn from such exchanges. And the mentor appreciates that I have done my homework before taking a bit of his or her valuable time.

Soon my husband and I will have the opportunity to make decisions about how best to preserve and grow his rollover and lump sum retirement from his previous job. We plan to turn our abject fear at this prospect into an action plan after educating ourselves by reading more books and listening to more tapes. Our strategy includes seeking out well-informed people and asking a lot of questions. Until the education takes place, we plan to emphasize preservation over growth.

I've found that the hardest part of making investments is going from thinking about doing them to actually doing them. At the same time I have also gained knowledge about banking and lending and how to open doors. There is abundant opportunity if one is willing to look for it and go after it.

Robert's rich dad was right. I also learned an extremely valuable lesson that is not taught in school: When it comes to the asset column nobody gives a darn about advanced degrees. For me, switching from the mind-set of "here's my academic résumé" to "here is my financial statement" was a life-changing event. Now I use those solid study skills that I acquired in medical school to process and absorb large amounts of financial materials.

Where my daughters are concerned, I've taken a bold step. After years of guiding them toward academic success and the Ivy League professional path, which their mother and father followed so diligently, I've made it clear that there is more than one road to financial freedom available to them. We talk to them about alternative means of income, and want them to know what their options are. They have the option of choosing a less exhausting path than the one we followed and they can learn to make money work for them early on.

Each daughter (one is now in college) keeps an investment account and understands the concept of compounded interest and growth because I arranged an appointment with a financial advisor for them. Instead of an allowance being handed to our younger daughter, she must learn to use the banking system and keep track of what she does—and doesn't—hold in her account. We are all learning together. They certainly are entitled to learn by trial and error, as we have.

Both of our daughters are encouraged to consider owning rental property early in life as a way to earn passive income. Their financial education will continue as they mature.

My mother also figures into the family equation. Optimally, a rent-free unit would be available to her. I am brainstorming to try to make that happen when the time comes.

My final challenge is facing the behavioral changes that I must make to be successful in this venture. That includes becoming smart with finances instead of overspending or avoiding facing the numbers, handling mail and business obligations efficiently instead of allowing a pile of unopened envelopes to collect on my desk, and scheduling business hours at home and actually being at the desk to complete the work instead of finding scores of excuses to be away at the appointed time. Like everything else, it's a learning process.

We Put Obstacles Up, We Can Take Them Down

Robert Kiyosaki writes about obstacles that hold people back. I think you can tell by now that fear was one of my big ones. Fear comes in all shapes and sizes. I was afraid that if I became successful with money, certain people would reject me. I was fearful of upsetting the balance of power within my marriage as I gained more control over our household affairs. Then, of course, there was my constant fear of appearing to be incompetent. Because of my education, many people assumed that I knew the answers to basic financial questions. They were wrong. I balanced my checkbook for the first time at age forty-six.

Then there were those bad habits. One terrible pattern was the feeling of being entitled to overspend—I even did it to prove to the occasional snooty waiter or desk clerk that they should not make financial assumptions about a person based on skin color. And there was the bad habit of placing the needs of others before my own well-being, which left me insufficient time to handle our business affairs.

The Next Lifestyle Change

Today, boosted by Rich Dad, I handle virtually 100 percent of our finances. In stark contrast to long-held feelings of financial insecurity and loss, I feel a tremendous sense of anticipation. I'm taking steps that will lead to the security of being financially free. At the same time I'm experiencing a profound sense of bonding with others who travel the financial freedom path.

For the first time in many years, I am passionately absorbed in this new agenda of financial and behavioral interests. And while there is much work to be done in acquiring and managing the assets that will grant us financial freedom, I'm excited about the future. But once I've achieved the "owning ten properties" goal, I can't imagine I'll stop—this is just too much fun!

More than ever, I believe that a person can recover from mistakes and learn a great deal from them. What a useful lesson I learned from Rich Dad—and I didn't have to go to school to learn it.

Chapter 6

Step Up to the Plate

REED J. SCHWEIZER
Wanatah, Indiana

For a long time I didn't understand money. Despite the fact that I earned a lot of it from the time I was twenty or so—I've always been a strictly commission-based salesman—keeping track of my bills and finances wasn't a high priority. Not surprisingly, most of my money problems stemmed from my own weakness. Overusing credit and letting myself become overextended got me into financial trouble repeatedly.

Lacking discipline to budget money properly, I never figured out a way to ride out the up-and-down fluctuations of income. Inevitably, the strain of unsteady salary got to me. Fears about being broke and consequently selling my product from a scared perspective led to dropping sales numbers. This unnerving cycle repeated over and over again.

Not until I chased my dream of getting into construction and real estate development did my income steady, and budgeting more effectively started coming naturally. I took the steps to catch my dream and turn it into reality and financial freedom. I believe that when you do what you love, the money follows. Discovering that passion started early.

The Union Ideal

The first twelve or thirteen years of my life my family was poor, which had a lot to do with the economy at the time. The recession of the late 1970s and the early 1980s halted a lot of construction and forced my hardworking father—he was a crane operator and a gung ho union member—out of a regular job. He would take whatever work he could find but it was still a hard time for us. Certainly my mother and two younger sisters and I had a roof over our heads and there was always enough food on the table. But we "shopped" at the Salvation Army instead of JCPenney. There were no extras; we squeaked by on the bare minimum.

When the recession finally ended, my father began to work steadily again, and life in our blue-collar household—we lived in northwest Indiana, near Lake Michigan—improved significantly.

But I never forgot what it was like to be poor. I recognized that working for someone else or a big company was not the solution to long-term money concerns. Even after my father went back to work full-time and started earning a really good salary, my parents, who budgeted and saved, didn't invest their money for a fundamental reason: They had absolutely no idea what to do. Their abiding belief was that his labor union would take care of us. The insurance policy, retirement funds, savings—everything was tied to the union. Interestingly enough, my pro-union dad never wanted me to follow in his footsteps. He recognized that he was trapped in an endless cycle of debt, spending, and total reliance on someone else for his own well-being as well as that of his family. But with a mortgage and four others to support, he couldn't justify doing something out of the ordinary with money. To him, that was too much of a risk.

At the same time a different way to live was in front of my eyes. My maternal grandfather owned a construction company. Financial stability oozed from him. It wasn't just his comfortable home, new cars, and a pocket that was always full of money. His total perspective was different because he didn't work for anyone else. He also donated a lot of money to the church, something that we couldn't afford to do.

In retrospect, I think my first inclination toward self-employment or becoming a business owner came from my grandfather's example. But my work ethic definitely comes from my dad.

Boy Businessman

I started working when I was in junior high school. I did the classic "kid with a mower" routine. After mowing one neighbor's lawn I would knock on the doors of the surrounding homes to generate more business. (More than a few of my friends thought I was nuts. "Why sweat more than you have to on a hot summer's day?" they asked. I ignored them and extra money filled my pockets.)

When I entered college it seemed like I would fulfill my parents' dream. After four years they figured I would graduate and be hired by a major corporation. The white-collar corporate world awaited me. I might even become a stockbroker. (Either that or play baseball for living. I was a catcher on the college baseball team and actually tried out for the Cleveland Indians and the Baltimore Orioles. Sad to say, I didn't make the cut.)

But deep down I wanted to be my own boss. Besides, knowing myself as I do, and my dislike of taking orders, I knew that a corporate job wouldn't work, either for me or for the company that hired me. I interviewed with recruiters who made it clear that at least my first two years as a novice stockbroker would be spent making cold calls.

My junior year I answered an ad for a sales job and eight months later I was doing really well. I owned a distributorship for a vacuum company. Buying inventory turned me into the owner. I oversaw two offices, trained the salespeople, and handled all the accounting. Not too shabby for a twenty-year-old.

After spending three years majoring in finance, I dropped out of school to manage the sales team I had built. The fact that I was also earning more than my professors was another incentive. My parents were disappointed that I didn't receive my diploma, although I did eventually earn an associate's degree in business management at a community college.

I was a very good salesman, but I didn't know much about running a business. I carried way too much responsibility. Sales were terrific but the bookkeeping was a nightmare. Sure, I was cash-rich but the eighty or more hours I put in a week were killing me and the taxes were murderous. Employees kept leaving.

Too immature to handle the money I made, let alone the business in general, I was in over my head and too proud to ask for help. Instead of seeking a consultant, an attorney, or an accountant, I tried to do everything on my own. I failed miserably. Eighteen months later, I gave up.

After that episode I owned both a construction business and a promotional product business. The first one, which lasted two years, I shared with a cousin. I learned another good lesson: I knew construction but I was not a skilled marketer. I started the second business after watching an infomercial that promoted the product. This venture lasted just a few months.

All in all I probably lost between $15,000 and $20,000 with these three ventures.

Unfortunately, I didn't pay much attention to the lessons of my first business failure. I repeated my pattern twice more, with the same results. Finally I learned that everyone in business needs professional help to keep everything legal and straight. No one can, or should, try to do everything. If you're a salesman, sell. Don't try to be an accountant or a lawyer or any other professional for which you aren't qualified. You'll only end up hurting yourself.

Fear Strikes Out

The next three years I was employed by a company that built and manufactured modular housing, a job in which I made a lot of money (and still didn't watch my finances). Then something happened which changed the way I regarded my job, my future, and, most of all, my fear.

Fear was a huge obstacle for me. Right about the time I bought *Rich Dad Poor Dad*, I got scared out of a deal that netted a guy I did some work for about $80,000. He paid me a $1,500 commission for helping him put the arrangement together.

Mentally I stepped back from the transaction because I realized something that hadn't occurred to me before. *I put the deal together! I knew what to do and how to do it but I was afraid of following through. By being afraid to take action it cost my family and me $80,000.* I couldn't believe it!

If I didn't need the $1,500 so bad, I would not even have cashed the check. It made me sick. I decided right then, that was it. From now on I was going to access the courage to pull the trigger on deals. Obviously I knew what to look for. It was time to reap the reward, not put the elements together for someone else to get rich. I saw others doing what I wanted to do, raking in tens of thousands every month off of the land that I wanted to buy. I was pumped to change.

About two months after reading *Rich Dad Poor Dad*, I started investing in real estate, because something so neat, so logical presented itself. After reading the book I think I was better able to recognize the opportunity. Clients came to the company I worked for all the time looking for land in a few specific areas in Indiana on which they wanted to build homes. The solution seemed so easy: *Purchase land where people wanted to buy land and sell it to them.*

The problem was that the two areas where customers desired to build homes only contained large parcels. Even though I had repeatedly brought this to the attention of the company I was working for, they did nothing about it. I did.

Here's How I Did It

I found out what steps would be required to take a large parcel, split it up, and sell off the pieces. It was easier than I imagined. My first project was a 5.1 acre piece of property in Chesterton, Indiana. I bought the ground from a family trust. This family had split the land into three lots years before so that other family members could have land to build on. Luckily for me, there were no engineering fees or surveying expenses. That saved me at least $3,000.

Even though the asking price was $90,000, my first offer was $45,000 because of the return I was looking for. I figured that I could get between $30,000 and $33,000 as sales prices for the lots, and I guess I was trying to hit a home run. Also, the payments on $45,000, about $300 a month until the lots would sell, were very manageable.

When the owners countered at $55,000 I wasn't scared a bit. I had already put a feeler out to a few of my customers to drive by, look at the property, and give me their thoughts. I told them that some lots might be coming available in that area, and if they did, would they be interested? Immediately one of my clients called back and said that the location was perfect. He said he would be willing to pay up to $31,000 for a lot in that area. That sealed the deal. I knew that I had to have that property.

Between the $31,000 and my 10 percent down payment from my own money, I would owe less than $20,000 on the remaining two lots, which were valued at $60,000. It was a no-brainer so I accepted the counteroffer of $55,000.

I found a one-year-interest-only loan at 4.75 percent because of the demand for property in that area. It was a very hot area, and I knew that I would have no problem selling off the lots. Also, the loan was renewable. At the end of the first year, if the lots were not sold, I could renew the loan at the current market interest rate. I sent in three interest payments totaling around $1,000.

Within six months I sold all the lots, appraised at $90,000, for $93,000. And even though I incurred $10,000 in unexpected sewer expenses, I earned $27,000 with virtually no effort. It's simple: $93,000 − $55,000 = $38,000 − $10,000 − $1,000 = $27,000.

My next investment was just as sweet. I called a real estate agent to ask her about something totally unrelated, and she asked me if I was in the market for any rental properties. Of course I said yes, and she went on to tell me about a little fixer-upper for $40,000. I went out to look at it and was not impressed. However, I *was* impressed with the forty-acre farm field that surrounded it. She had them both listed and it turned out that the same person owned both properties. The asking price was $40,000 for the house with two acres, and $200,000 for the remaining thirty-eight acres, a total of $240,000.

My initial offer was $150,000 for the whole package. I knew that the lady who used to live in the house had died, and it was probably an estate deal. The owner countered with $200,000 for the land only. I came back with $160,000 for the whole package, and they countered once again, this time at $170,000. I was floored! I had just bought a small house and forty acres for $170,000!

This time the financing was considerably tougher. I had to come up with the 30 percent down payment. I had just made some money, but I didn't have $51,000. I thought about Robert saying that he was not allowed to say "I can't afford it" around his rich dad, so I had to think, "How can I afford it?"

I talked to a banker friend of mine who joined me as a partner, and we came up with the down payment and bought the land. We spent about $5,000 on soil tests and surveys, and in seven months sold seven of the ten lots for a total of $229,000. As a result there is $50,000 in our account and we don't owe a dime on the last three lots, which still carry a total asking price of $103,000.

When it's all said and done, we should both make in the neighborhood of $80,000 on the project!

We paid about $3,000 in interest during the duration of our loan. We broke the properties into pieces that ranged from two to ten acres with asking prices between $28,000 and $54,000.

The house was in terrible condition, so we tore it down, and sold the lot for $28,000. In retrospect, that may have been a mistake because there was no passive income. My partner and I disagreed about what to do with the house. I wanted to rehab it, rent it out, or just try to sell it. He talked me out of it, which we regret now. But since our biggest mistake created $28,000, I don't think we screwed up too badly. We still profited about $19,000 from the sale of that lot. I wish all of my screw-ups netted me that much money. ($28,000 − $4,250 per acre for a two-acre lot = $19,500 profit.)

Recently I accepted offers on the remaining three lots, so here's the total breakdown:

Land:	$170,000
Soil tests/surveys:	$5,000
Interest:	$3,000
House tear-down:	$1,000
Total costs:	$179,000
Total of lots selling price:	$323,000
−Total costs:	$179,000
Profit:	$144,000

We closed on this land just about a year ago. I have put less than twenty hours' worth of work into this project. My cut is $72,000, which works out to be about $3,600 per hour. The value of my free time is priceless when you think of how long it would have taken me to earn $72,000 at an hourly rate.

Unfortunately, the company where I worked looked at my real estate investments as a conflict of interest. I was selling the homes that would be built on the land I owned. So after about six months of selling property to my customers, as well as those of other salespeople, I figured that it was time to leave.

Within six months I found a job at another company that builds houses. This organization allows me to set my own schedule, and encourages and even helps me to invest in land. Technically I'm a subcontractor, which allows me to come and go as I see fit, and it gives me the free time to take my investing to the next level. I jumped at the opportunity to switch to the new company.

My current project is a great one. A friend of mine in the housing business called me a couple of months ago with an opportunity. One of his customers owned eight acres he needed to get rid of because of a divorce. The client thought that the land could hold three lots due to local zoning. I did a little research and discovered that four of the eight acres actually fell within the city limits. This meant I could actually get six lots out of the property due to differences in the amount of required road frontage.

The asking price was $50,000. My initial offer was $25,000. He didn't even counter. I waited two weeks and called him back to reiterate the bid. The divorce had heated up and he really needed to get rid of the holding right away. I raised my offer to $30,000, with a commitment to close the deal in two weeks. The time frame really appealed to him. Two weeks later I paid $30,000 in cash, which I had because of the previous two investments. (Since we had the money from the previous deals in our account, we decided to pay cash. I know that not leveraging this property goes against some Rich Dad principles, but the seller was in a jam, needed quick cash, and I was happy to help him out. If we needed the cash back out of the property, it would have been easy to do through an equity loan, so we just paid cash.)

The six lots carried a total asking price of $120,000. After less than a month, I received an offer on the first lot. We have sold two lots for a total of $35,800 and we still own four more lots at $17,900 each. Without interest payments, and adding in surveying fees of around $2,500, this should make me approximately $74,900 with less than ten hours of my time and effort invested in the project.

My partner and I recently bought a three-bedroom, one-bathroom investment house. We paid $46,500 in cash and put in less than $5,000 in repairs. We received an offer within five days of putting it on the market for $88,900 and wrote a contract within two weeks after that.

I have made around $100,000 on the sales, but more importantly I own nine lots free and clear totaling $223,000. Pumped to do more, I am looking at a deal that would give me forty-four lots to sell on a fifty-six-acre piece of ground. Hopefully the deals will keep getting larger as my financial strength grows.

Currently I am self-employed as a housing consultant, and I'm minding my own business, which sells land. I plan to own my own sales center next year that will provide one-stop shopping to home buyers. Customers will be able to pick their lot of land, the style of their modular home, and apply for a mortgage at the same convenient place. Every aspect of the transaction will generate cash.

Once You Start It's Impossible to Stop

One of my goals for this year is to design and build a mini-mall building in a subdivision that is going up near me. The subdivision will contain 400 new homes, an apartment complex, and a lot of duplexes. Within two miles there is a college campus and two enormous trailer parks. It seems obvious to me that this area is ripe for a six- or seven-unit mini-mall building containing a pizzeria, a liquor store, and a beauty shop among other goods and services. I plan on acquiring two buildings containing three or four rental storefronts.

Within five years my goal is to raise my passive income up to $10,000 a month along with being free of bad debt. Buying three rental properties a year for the next few years should accomplish that. At that point I will be thirty-five years old, my wife will be thirty-three, and our son will be six. I'll feel comfortable about retirement and take a year off, reflect on my achievements, and plan for the future. Being with my family as much as I want is a terrific goal. Then I will be ready to shift into high gear and invest in companies before they go public or even help them go public.

When I look back at where I was just a year ago the difference is staggering. I was stuck in a high-paying job that was going nowhere. I was chained to an office from 9:00 A.M. to 7:00 P.M. five days a week but customers only sat across from me two or three hours of that time. It was such a drag. Now I am free to scout out properties. I can get up in the morning and hang out with my son, help people buy homes, go to job sites to check progress, and generally enjoy my day. The whole world is my customer because I own land.

Best of all, fear no longer blips on my radar screen. Achieving success took care of it. I am now confident that I know a good deal when I see one because of my achievements. It's like playing ball. When you've gotten a hit, you're not scared to be at the plate. Investing in real estate is no different. Once you've tasted a little success you want to keep going, get another hit and drive it further than it went the last time.

Step Up to the Plate

The person who steps forward and takes a chance is the one who stands out. I believe that we live in the greatest country in the world with the maximum opportunities for riches in the history of the world. If you don't take advantage of what is out there you'll regret it. So take a swing at being financially free. Even if you fail the first time you always get another chance. In baseball, you get three strikes before you're out—and even then you get another turn. You just have to wait a bit. One thing is certain: You miss every swing you don't take.

Chapter 7

The Root of All That Is Good

Dan McKenzie
Greensboro, North Carolina

Money is the root of all evil. That's what I was raised to believe. The only people who possessed money were neurotics, crooks, the scourge of humanity, or a depraved combination of all three. These beliefs, which were deeply entrenched in my close, large family, and voiced with certainty by my highly cynical father, left a deep mark. Apparently once humans stopped being hunters and gatherers, we started marching toward doom and gloom. The more successful you were, the more immersed into the educational and political system you became, the more brainwashed you were. Financial success, instead of being regarded as an accomplishment, was akin to being sucked into hell. There was no greater stupidity than deluding yourself and wasting your time thinking about money. Doing so literally damned you for all eternity.

Obviously, a pretty major obstacle to financial awareness, much less success, stood in my way. I knew there was a lot to learn, but I lacked mentors. No close friends or associates who managed to leap over the wall to financial freedom were in my immediate circle of influence. Most daunting of all, I held no clear or consistent direction of what to do with money or how to earn it.

Learning by trial and error was a necessity. Two steps forward, three steps back became my pattern. More than a few times my experiences seemed to validate the convictions drummed into my head.

Most people have so thoroughly accepted themselves as they are, they give little or no thought as to how they got that way. But as the fifth child of eight in my family—or maybe because of it—that was not my case. I tried to overcome fear, cynicism, and negativity very early on in life and I wanted to find my own path. I often wondered why some people seemed to have everything and others went through life with the barest of necessities. Intimately familiar with the latter, I wanted to experience the former. Maybe my father was right, but I wanted to find out for myself.

I thought working hard was the answer. While most of my classmates were playing sports or participating in extracurricular school activities, I flipped donuts for $1.50 an hour before and after class my last couple of years of high school. From the get-go, I knew that being an employee was not for me but I didn't know what to do about it or how. After I graduated I learned a trade and became a cabinetmaker who fashioned high-end pieces. But after the business went from producing custom fine woodworking to mass-produced particle board and Formica boxes I became disenchanted.

Moving on, I was employed by several highly successful businesses in my small Ohio hometown but ended up quitting each one. Many friends were quick to voice their ridicule. After all, what was I thinking, leaving "great" jobs others wanted so badly?

As it happened, a bigger concern was taking over my attention. During the course of every job I held I sat down with a notepad and calculated my expenses and what my projected income would be twenty years hence. Even with raises, nothing seemed to change much. No matter how terrific the job was, after expenses I still couldn't figure out how I was going to live the life I desired—even with the best of pay raises. It was during these introspective sessions that I would see my father's face and hear his words: "You are wasting your time . . . you can't beat the system, give up . . ." Like a bad song I couldn't get out of my head, his chronic negativity just played over and over. What else could I do? Drop out of society like he had and live like a hermit? No, I had already become happily discontented with that lifestyle. I wanted to experience what having money felt like. At that point I made up my mind I wanted to:

1. Be a millionaire by the time I turned thirty.
2. Travel the world.
3. Own two houses, one in the United States and one overseas.
4. Meet Farrah Fawcett (after all, this was the 1970s).

There was a big problem to confront as a result of my decision: I felt lost and without direction, despite the talent I knew I possessed. I had nowhere to turn. Nonetheless, I hunted for job after job, advancing in my career via trial and error until I attained positions normally held by college graduates. I had wanted to attend college but I ended up far too busy traveling the world to find the time to sit in classrooms for four years. By the time my high school classmates finished their "higher" education, I had been to, or through, over fifty countries and hundreds of international cities.

While it was not apparent to me at that time, the effect the travel was having on me was an exposure to numerous groups and individuals with positive motivation or success habits. The contact with these types of positive life patterns helped me to discover a distinct contrast between success consciousness and status quo routines.

When asked where I attended college, I always told people (and still do) that I attended UHK (University of Hard Knocks), where I received a degree in Results. I learned by doing.

But still I found no peace or resolution to my income dilemma. There seemed to be an eerie connection between the jobs experience and what my father had been attempting to instill. But neither one made an apparent significant connection: The size of the success you want to build is dependent solely upon the amount of personal power you are willing to give. How and what a person can contribute to others is based on what he feels about himself. I began to grasp that there were two distinct mind-sets. My father's mind-set (guided by habit rather than intellect) could only think in terms of hoarding or receiving (scarcity) and was exclusively negative-oriented. His obsession was conserving "what was his" versus finding or creating value for others. I was slowly becoming aware that there was another mind-set, one that thinks in terms of creating or adding value (abundance/giving) and is highly positive. By seeking ways to offer more of my full potential—and talent—I not only could create more value, but also achieve an inner vitality. As an employee I didn't feel that I was making contributions that were as meaningful or significant as they could be. Remembering the hunter-gatherer ideal of my childhood, I realized that the problem with living such a "simple" life was that it didn't entail giving anything back. The necessity to contribute something useful was missing. When the only goal is money, there are so many different ways of obtaining it that a person can become confused as to what avenue to take. Money is merely a means to an end, not the end. It was my father's view of money being the end that I was beginning to unravel.

I worked as an employee from 1974 to 1987 and then transitioned into a business owner, but still not by some master understanding or clear plan. One of my countless blessings is a curious mind and after many years of feeling disenfranchised, I decided to take a leap of faith and start my own company. I quit my "secure" job at a Fortune 100 aerospace company, at the height of its success, where I earned more money than I dreamed possible. Once again, I took a lot of ribbing from my colleagues, all of whom were MBAs, Ph.D.'s, and the like. They thought I was either to be pitied—because I was doomed to fail—or mocked, for the same reason.

At the age of twenty-eight I not only had learned to overcome the cynicism and negativity of family, friends, and co-workers, but I was also able to begin forming new life patterns which conformed more to the life I desired. I began a new journey to controlling my own destiny.

Self-Control Reaps Rewards

Several months after *Rich Dad Poor Dad* came out, my second oldest brother (one of five brothers and two sisters) told me about it. Here was a book that was putting into words what I was struggling with almost my entire life. All of a sudden a new definition of what I was doing came to light. After reading *Rich Dad's CASHFLOW Quadrant* I realized that by having started my own company I was already operating on the right side as a business owner and investor, rather than as employee or self-employed on the left side of the Quadrant.

What an incredible liberating and wonderful feeling! Finally, my day of emancipation was at hand. At last, a sense of peace with all I had been doing up to that point came over me.

One example of my focus on the right side of the Quadrant (which is called "The Fast Track" in the game CASHFLOW) was after I quit my aerospace job.

Tired of paying rent since the age of eighteen—it just didn't make sense to spend $400 to $800 a month and gain nothing from it—I bought a three-acre tract of land thirty minutes south of Austin, Texas. I figured that I could build a structure on the land and live there. I didn't even care if it was a shack. I calculated if I paid X, and eventually sold it for Y, I would come out okay. It was pure "blind risk."

The man who owned the property was desperate to sell it. To pay cash for the property—$12,000, a huge amount for me at the time—I sold my fancy sports car and wiped out my savings. Next I spent my evenings and weekends building a modest house on the property. I lived there awhile before I sold the property for $75,000 and used the proceeds to start my first company.

(I built that company, which provided engineering services and products for all the major airlines around the world, into a multimillion-dollar business within three years, two years and millions of dollars ahead of my goal. I also did it without borrowing a dime.)

But post–Rich Dad, my approach to real estate buying, as well as my view of myself, underwent a fundamental shift. Pre–Rich Dad, my purchases were about trying to amass huge amounts of cash so as to not have to borrow too much money. In hindsight I missed many wonderful opportunities. If I couldn't put enough money down to make the property affordable for my own "earned" income monthly cashflow, then I would just pass on the deal.

I had been sufficiently subjugated where borrowing was concerned: Debt of any kind was bad. "Never owe anyone anything!" was another one of my father's core BS (belief system) statements. Not having a clue that there was such a thing as good debt, I did my best (in my father's eyes) to not borrow any money to buy the land for my first house, much less build it. This was a deep behavioral pattern to overcome. Thanks to Rich Dad this has been probably the most profound fundamental paradigm shift I have experienced related to money.

Learning something new takes time because thinking while acting is necessary. But as I accumulated small successes I slowly chipped away at the fears, phobias, inhibitions, and negative influences that were implanted when I was a child. The successes took the form of new habits, specifically how I thought about things. At its most basic level I traded negative thinking patterns for positive thought patterns. I don't believe a price can be put on what that is worth!

Prior to Rich Dad, I never saw the cashflow portion of the equation. I can honestly say I never looked at property as a money generator. Now, it became literally a whole new means to evaluate not only property, but assets in general. What a powerful, liberating, and invaluable distinction! Thank you, Rich Dad!

Instead of flying by the seat of my pants, I had direction and control. It was as if a light went on in a dark room.

Here's How I Did It

I've made many real estate investments and I attribute my success to always doing my homework in doing the due diligence on the property and seeking to ensure that I am making a smart decision (informed risk instead of blind risk) prior to purchasing a property. I think that a lot of people become either a little overwhelmed or fearful when there is more than one issue to consider. Most of my seeming long shots involved a good deal of judgment and paying attention to trends or value not necessarily obvious because they involved appreciating more than one variable. I have been building a database for all the possible uses of real estate. I break down both commercial uses and residential uses. Then I evaluate the needs based on the area and determine what makes sense. I use my spreadsheets to calculate costs-to-income potential as well as how the real estate costs impact each of the various niche uses. Next I look at other examples of how similar solutions have been done and figure out if there is some way to improve on those instances to create more value. In other words, I look at what can drive the sales side of the equation and then look at what will drive the cost side of the equation. The simple version of how I do my homework is this: I determine who, what, how, when, where, and why.

Here's an example. About eighteen months after a deep crash hit the real estate market in central Texas, I purchased seventy acres along a small east–west highway that connected two major north–south highways just outside Austin.

My offer price—$3,200 an acre (they had received offers of $7,000 before the crash and wouldn't sell) seemed risky and high to many friends and acquaintances that had already lost their shirts in the crash. Even my banker asked me repeatedly if I was sure that I wanted to pay that price. But I knew that the major highways weren't going to disappear and the connection between them was still going to be important. When the economy turned around, building would commence in the direction of those seventy acres. Still, I realized that land was not an asset because it is typically negative cash-flow. Nonetheless, I wanted to work out how I could secure the land and pay for it while waiting for a few key issues to change. My emotions were polar opposites. Sometimes I felt excited when I focused on upside potential but then I was saddened as a result of everyone thinking I was nuts for even considering buying it.

The property had both highway frontage on the front side and views and river frontage on the back side. Being smack dab in the midway point between the only north and south major arteries was important. But all of this aside, I paid attention to the issue of drinking water, or rather the lack of it, which was one of the issues affecting the value of much of the properties along this corridor. In this specific example, knowing development potential was limited by the lack of affordable drinking water, my attention and focus shifted to *who* would be a likely candidate to solve that issue? (That is, *who* would benefit from solving it?) *When* would that person be able to solve it? *How* would he solve it? Water co-op? City annexation? Individual wells? (*Which* solution would make the most financial sense?)

Since there was no public water available along this five-mile stretch of land, and wells would require extreme depths with no guarantee of either water quality or volume, the large plots were not considered usable for residential developments within any reasonable price range. However, my awareness of this problem allowed me to explore what, if anything, could be done to remedy the water problem. I discovered that a large development group wanted to put a private golf course, with upper-end homes, 500 feet further down the road on the opposite side from the property I acquired. They were challenged with the water issue as well. I learned that they were making a deal with both the city and the only water co-op around to ensure that a water supply would be available.

Armed with this knowledge, I felt that the property values of development purposes would be impacted positively when the water lines were in place. This turned out to be true. The land values more than quadrupled as a result of this one issue! Taking the time to determine if and when and by whom the water problem would be addressed changed the "risk" from "blind" to "informed."

After several years the area returned to growth brought on by many high-tech companies moving into the area. Real estate began to climb again. Growth pushed property prices up to $14,000 to $25,000 an acre.

In the meantime, I began to employ six basic criteria to evaluate and shop property:

1. *Motivation* (either the seller's or mine). Take the case of the seventy-acre parcel, which was not even on the market. I had already picked the property based on location and growth trends I was compiling. Then I researched the owners and visited them to evaluate their relationship to the property and how the potential changes would or would not affect them. It turned out that three sisters had inherited the land years before. Now the two surviving sisters, who were both around eighty years old, weren't interested in keeping the property any longer. At that stage of their lives, money was more important to them. But there was more to factor into the deal. The sisters first said no to my offer. Undeterred, I tried again and talking to them found out that they didn't want the land to be developed. With that understanding, I informed them about my intentions, that I did not intend to develop the land the way others did (i.e., building homes one on top of the other). Based on their responses, I knew we would be able to do a deal that would work out for everyone's benefit. *I think this is one of the most critical and important issues associated to any piece of real estate.*

The property had to meet my criteria. Then what the sellers wanted had to be considered.

2. *Condition of the property.* This goes beyond whether it was just good or bad, or whether it was raw or landscaped. I had to develop a fairly good head for what was and wasn't significant, along with lots of clever ideas for alternate cost issues as well as a clear idea about zoning options (i.e., zoned for commercial, residential, or other use). For instance, a lovely vista showcasing rolling hills or a river or an orchard can be significant. Views matter to lots of people.

3. *Terms.* What the seller, the bank, and I wanted. Taking into account number one and number two, terms can be altered to accommodate everyone involved.

4. *Location.* I know this has been beaten to death, but location, when lined up with growth trends (new roads, businesses, population shifts, and

so on), presents many possibilities that may not be immediately apparent. For instance, scoping out a particular area showed me that demand for land was moving in that direction.

5. *Price*. There's nothing like buying a great "retail" property at a "wholesale" price. But as with all the above, there are many more issues related to price.

6. *Relationships*. This is what Rich Dad refers to as networks. Talk to people; listen to what they are saying. Tips about upcoming areas (I found out that Dell Computer was planning to build in a certain area, which meant people looking for rental properties, new homes, and places to shop) are often conveyed during casual conversations.

The following are three recent property purchases in Austin. While gaining yearly cashflow from them, based on my projections my equity may grow to more than $310,000 over the course of five years. Even better, one of the three is located at what will be a future key intersection as the result of two critical real estate changes in the area. The first is that the local airport is expanding to add a new runway. This changes a major highway routing, which will bring it right past the property. I have already received offers to sell the property for double what I paid for it.

Here's the breakdown on the first property, a single-family dwelling I paid $134,000 for:

Cash invested into property

Down payment:	$28,350
Closing costs paid by me:	$1,200
Repairs/renovations paid by me:	$6,200
	$35,750

Monthly cashflow analysis

Rental income:	$960
— Vacancy loss (5%):	$48
Total income:	$912

Monthly expenses:	
— Taxes (property) and insurance:	$117.91
— Repairs/maintenance:	$41.67
— Management fee (10% of rents):	$96

– Loan payment (5-year renewable balloon notes at 5.25%)	$605.37
(All other expenses are paid by the tenants.)	
	$860.95
Net monthly cashflow:	$51.05

Cash-on-cash return

Annual cashflow ($51.05 × 12)	$612.60
÷	
Amount of cash put into property	$35,750
Cash-on-cash return	1.7%

Note: This is not a large return on my investment but I have the potential for capital gains if I choose to sell the property later.

Similar properties in the area are selling for $175,000.

The second property, also a single-family house, cost me $128,000.

Cash put into property

Down payment:	$24,500
Closing costs paid by me:	$6,000
Repairs/renovations paid by me:	$0
	$30,500

Monthly cashflow analysis

Rental income:	$1,123.20
– Vacancy loss (5%)	56.16
Total income:	$1,067.04

Monthly expenses:	
– Taxes (property) and insurance:	$179.58
– Repairs/maintenance:	$41.66
– Management fee (10% of rents):	$112.32
– Loan payment (5-year renewable balloon notes at 5.25%):	$635.58
(All other expenses are paid by the tenants.)	
	$969.14
Net monthly cashflow:	$97.90

Cash-on-cash return

Annual cashflow ($97.90 × 12)	$1,174.80
÷	
Amount of cash put into property	$30,500
Cash-on-cash return	3.8%

Similar properties in the area are selling for $145,000.

Another terrific source of monthly cashflow came from buying an airplane hangar and associated executive office complex. The hangar contained rental space; corporate aircraft owners could safely park their very expensive jets inside. Each owner would pay approximately $600 to $1,000 per month based on the size of the aircraft. With an average of ten aircraft per building we were generating about $8,000 gross income per month (about $96,000 a year) for a property that I was able to purchase for less than $250,000.

I rented the office building to a professional engineering firm (which also happened to be my first business) and generated an additional $4,000 per month ($48,000 a year) of rent on a mortgage of $125,000 for the offices. (By the way, I grew this business to $7 million in annual sales before selling it.)

After paying expenses and debt, these two properties threw off a monthly cashflow of $4,300. The cashflow from these properties not only paid for them, they covered my personal expenses as well.

Out of the five businesses I began I still own two: a technology consulting company focused primarily on small- to medium-size businesses, and my new, high-tech company, which is an innovative community-based advertising and communication system. Reading *Protecting Your #1 Asset* by Michael Lechter, one of the Rich Dad's advisors, taught me that I needed to safeguard this intellectual property.

My goal for this year is to get my latest business going so that it spins off positive cashflow by the end of year. Five years from now my target is monthly cashflow somewhere between $50,000 and $80,000.

Change Your Perspective, Change Your Life

At the deepest level, I believe the greatest gift of the Rich Dad information is the restoration of imagination and motivation lost through hopelessness and negativity. Consider this: If the dream of financial comfort seems so out of the realm of reality because time and again a person has been disillusioned, that person will give up hope of ever attaining that dream.

Unfortunately as it relates to money and finance, all of us are surrounded with more negative people than we are with positive. Sadly, with constant negative reinforcement, imagination, the visualization of what could be, narrows until it disappears. Over time this exposure creates a pessimistic veneer that influences your thinking, your acting, and what you can achieve. When it does, motivation is lost because there is nothing to push toward. Without imagination nothing can be achieved. If your mind is not bringing in good constructive ideas it is because of bad mental habits. I believe the Rich Dad information bridges the gap between the despair of disappointment and the hope for accomplishment by shifting the influence from negative to positive. It allows you to create, or re-create, an internal picture of what could be— and helps to propel you toward it. Fear of what a person can't do is replaced by a positive image of what a person can do.

I also believe that the intermediary between ignorance and a commodity is the development and refinement of a systematic replicable way of performing a task. When viewed from this perspective, the Rich Dad group has moved the understanding of value creation closer to a commodity then any group before.

One of the most significant benefits I've received from the Rich Dad materials is a renewed view of life. In my experience, my passion has been reignited and I understand how my life continues to be changed. I've learned to find new opportunities as the world shifts from an industrial economy to an information economy. Financial freedom is a reality. Hope for a better future exists.

I experienced firsthand one of the most powerful examples of this. My oldest brother, who moved out west years ago and owned his own business, and I weren't close. (Not because of personal differences, just a result of our large family and our age differential.) On a recent visit I asked him to indulge me and read *Rich Dad Poor Dad*. I bought him a copy and handed it to him. We were in my car, and he started leafing through it. Then he stopped, and started reading aloud. As he put it, he had read books about economics but didn't really understand how money worked.

He connected to what he was reading and he connected to me in a way we never experienced before. Now we had a common language at our disposal.

We shared what I had already undergone on my own: a profoundly positive shift from what I had to what I would like to have. By being able to share our view of how we wanted our lives to be, we bridged our personal gap along with our personal financial ones.

I don't know anyone who does not have challenges. Everyone can tell stories of personal traumas. Holding thoughts of inadequacy, lack, gloom, and ill will doesn't do anyone any good. You cannot hold a picture of failure and expect it to guide you to success. But, if we choose to do so, we can use these experiences to propel us forward instead of using them as excuses not to achieve our dreams. The most sobering thought I can share about money as a result of my exposure to and influence by the Rich Dad materials is that a person must constantly be creating, finding, or adding value. Money in and of itself has no conscience. It cares nothing about personal history, excuses, or life challenges. If a person does not add value to his or her life, eventually and one way or the other, money will flow to those who do!

And while I've accomplished much of what I set out to do (okay, I still haven't met Farrah!), I'm in my mid-forties and confident about doing much more. My primary concern is the ultimate freedom of being able to contribute my core passion to society. It's become apparent to me that having money is not the big thrill. It is being able to step back and look at the value I've manifested in exchange for the money—that's where the real emotional satisfaction is. And that, I feel, is the root of all good.

Part III

A Different Focus

One of my strongest personal beliefs is that you become what you study. If you gain knowledge of the law, you can become a lawyer. If you study history, you can become a historian. But no matter what subjects you did or did not learn, if you study how to invest to create cashflow, you can become financially free. Then you can decide if you want to continue with what you've been trained to do, retire, or begin to study something entirely new. That's what financial freedom can do for you.

Many men and women, at different stages in their lives, have told me how studying the Rich Dad information helped them to redefine themselves and change their lives.

In this section you'll meet Tom Kotula, who lives in Minnesota. A man who toiled at a dead-end job for years, never getting ahead of the bills, and putting in a lot of overtime hours that stole time away from his family, Tom seemed stuck. An employee without money, he felt strongly that making a change was crucial, for himself and his family. Once he began his financial education with Rich Dad he discovered that not having money is no obsta-

cle to making investments and creating cashflow. If you've ever felt stuck in a job, and stayed there because you felt there was no choice, read Tom's story and become inspired.

Then there's Wade and Carol Yamamoto. They live in Hawaii, which is where I grew up. When we first met them, Carol, a teacher, had already become involved with network marketing but her husband had not. How they came to terms and decided what was best for both of them is a terrific example of understanding and focusing on what is important to both people. Their story underlines the significance of a couple studying and working together to reach the same goal, the sacrifices that goal requires, and the incredible results it can give. Their story not only illustrates a very common worry that I hear about frequently, namely, "What will our family or friends or neighbors think?," but also shows how this clear-thinking duo overcame it. Rich Dad–inspired teamwork begins at home.

You'll also read about Merced Hall, her husband, Jeff Hall, and Jeff's identical twin brother, Jon Hall. They live in Utah. Their story is a Gen-X saga of great expectations dashed when they were forced to face an unexpected predicament after college. It offers a keen insight into the particular troubles of a well-educated group that marched out of universities with degrees into temporary high-paying, high-stress jobs at dot.coms and prestigious corporations that promised much, delivered little, and took away a lot more.

At the very beginning of what they thought were promising careers—everything they had been told was worth studying and competing for—they discovered that being employees didn't suit them. It wasn't that they were lazy or uncommitted. Merced, Jeff, and Jon realized that they didn't want to work for someone else for the next three or four decades. They wanted financial independence and they wanted to take control of their lives to make that happen.

Instead of wasting time trying to convince themselves that they "should do" something that wasn't right for them because they spent so much time and effort to receive excellent grades and impressive degrees, they studied the Rich Dad information and then took steps to begin investing. Positive cashflow to gain financial security was their goal. Fully admitting that there were more than a few scary moments, they persevered. Just as my rich dad teaches, they made mistakes, learned from them, and moved on to create successes.

Even more importantly, they sent a strong message to their peers who may find themselves disappointed in their demanding jobs or who expected to cash out of start-up companies in just a few years. These three didn't complain about what happened. Instead, they took honest stock of who they were, educated themselves in a whole new way, and using that solid foundation changed their lives. As opposed to feeling burned-out and cynical, they grasped new possibilities and took action.

Ken Hobson, who lives in Pennsylvania, has another story to tell. Well established in his field, Ken earned a very good living for many years but felt that something was missing. For him, studying the Rich Dad information gave him the means to find that missing piece. He found a way to combine his investments with his new work. Instead of worrying about what will happen when he chooses to retire, he is confident of building increasing monthly cashflow. And he is having fun in the process.

Tom, Wade, Carol, Merced, Jeff, Jon, and Ken didn't wait for "something to happen" to them. They took charge of their lives and altered them for the better. Not happy with the situations they found themselves in, they made the conscious decision to move toward financial security. They didn't let time-worn excuses get in their way, nor did they listen to people who questioned their actions (and, I'm willing to guess, their sanity).

As an alternative to buying into the conventional wisdom of staying put ("The devil you know is better than the devil you don't") and not trying something new ("You've never done that before. How do you know it will work?"), they made their plans, did their research, found the support they needed among each other—and succeeded. They studied how to become financially free and started taking action.

Chapter 8

Better Than Winning the Lottery

THOMAS G. KOTULA
St. Cloud, Minnesota

For seven and a half years I toiled in a dead-end job sorting mail at the post office. I logged overtime hours whenever I could—like evenings, weekends, and holidays—to earn a few extra dollars. With bills due, there was no choice. My wife and I lived from one payday to the next. Often I worked a second job and also put in overtime at whatever I was doing: driving a school bus, delivering pizza, performing odd jobs at a golf course—the list goes on. I don't recall a single job that was satisfying. What I lacked was motivation to make a change. I also lacked faith in myself. I thought that my lack of experience would hold me back. That, coupled with a tendency to procrastinate, was the obstacle facing me.

Eighteen months ago, before I discovered the tools and hope to change our lives, my bank account was essentially empty. When I allowed myself to think about retirement, I figured that the post office would require nineteen more years of my reluctant presence before I could collect a pension. My post office retirement account, filled with mutual funds, was our sole investment. The future didn't look too bright for us.

Today, thanks to Rich Dad, our bank account contains about $90,000 and we're secure enough financially that I could literally get by for ten or more years without a job if I chose to do so. I'm a Navy veteran who studied speech and management at college for three years. Thirty-three years old, I'm the father of a three-year-old son. I plan to retire by the time I'm forty.

A Fresh Look at an Old Subject

Thinking about different ways to make money has always been a hobby of mine. In the past I tried a few small businesses. One, which I shared with a partner, was a bar toy. The person playing would try to flip quarters into a little hole in the toy and win a prize. My partner lost about $2,000 and I broke even. Yet this venture was a big step for me. Forced to talk to lots of people, I faced rejection and learned to deal with it.

Books about real estate and finance were always interesting to me, too. I started reading them in 1988, when I joined the Navy. Although I found real estate to be a fascinating subject, I never considered buying any. Nonetheless, when I heard about *Rich Dad Poor Dad* I bought a copy. After I read it I went back for three more books in the series. When I was laid up last year recovering from knee surgery and saw Robert's infomercial on television, I ordered the *Choose to Be Rich* series.

Rich Dad Poor Dad was the most beneficial book I had ever read because of Robert's philosophy. First, he stressed that opportunities are out there. Then he pointed out that one isn't necessarily better than another. But what really spoke to me was his outlook on the value of real estate. Living off the income that real estate generated, instead of using it to supplement existing income, was a possibility I hadn't considered.

Thinking in terms of how large real-estate-invested dollars could grow gave me a different outlook and certainly got me started. And I have no intention of stopping.

Here's How I Did It

Shortly after reading *Rich Dad Poor Dad*, a set of timely circumstances led me to buy my first rental property in a St. Cloud suburb. My sister, the mother of a three-year-old, longed to move out of her cramped apartment. Living in a town of 60,000 plus 14,000 college kids who attend St. Cloud

State, I knew that rentals were abundant. However, this was the first time I realized that those spaces were potentially valuable to me.

After three months of speaking to real estate agents and asking them if they handled rental properties, I found a triplex that worked for my sister and myself. The asking price was $99,000; I offered $94,000 with $5,000 coming back to me at closing. Because my sister qualified for a first-time homeowner loan, and because she planned to live in one of the units, we were able to get 100 percent financing, at 7 percent for thirty years, for the $99,000 mortgage. This was important, since neither of us had any spare cash for a down payment.

I took care of collecting the rental fees while my sister looked after the common area and the outside. Even with the reduced rent paid by my sister, the house turned over $300 in passive cashflow a month, an amount she and I share. Here's the breakdown:

Cash put into property

Down payment:	$0
Closing costs paid by us:	$0
Repairs/renovations paid by us:	$6,000
	$6,000

Monthly cashflow analysis

Rental income:	$1,365
Monthly expenses:	
—Taxes (property):	$50
—Insurance:	$40
—Repairs/maintenance:	$0
—Heat and electric:	$150
—Trash collection and water:	$65
—Reserve:*	$0
—Loan payment (30 years at 7%):	$760
	$1,065

*All of our cashflow is going into the reserve.

Net monthly cashflow:	$300

Cash-on-cash return

Annual cashflow ($300 × 12)	$3,600
÷	
Amount of cash put into property	$6,000
Cash-on-cash return:	60%

My sister and I bought the property in September 2001, and by November I was investigating other ways to own rentals. There was another factor. The triplex we purchased needed a lot of repairs. Because I have a real aversion to doing a lot of work I know nothing about we were forced to hire a lot of help. Like Robert, I don't fix toilets.

However, we recently refinanced the mortgage at 4.5 percent for thirty years and our passive income rose to $650 a month. We pulled $25,000 out from the refinance and split the proceeds. Even with $6,000 in repairs, we each walked away with about $10,000. I plan to invest the money in more real estate. We still own the property and it currently cashflows $250 per month.

This was a terrific start but after a few months I realized that other plans were necessary in order for me to get where I wanted to be, namely forever gone from my post office job and on the road to financial security. To do that I began to look for real estate that I could build on. Within a day I located three acres in a small town close by that was zoned for multifamily dwellings. I decided to build five twin homes, which contained two single-family dwellings each.

It took a lot of research to do the job, but it was well worthwhile. Keep in mind I still had no money to invest with. But I knew what to do and that gave me a big advantage. As Robert always says, you need to do your homework. And that's exactly what I did. I knew there were a lot of ways to get a job done. All that was required was the commitment to keep searching for the right formula.

I wrote out a list of questions that needed to be answered, studied financing from books, and queried people and grabbed the Yellow Pages. My primary goal was getting a loan. I called up banks and mortgage companies just to ask them questions that I was wondering about. Those queries included:

- What types of loans they offered.
- If they provided loans for new construction.
- What type of down payment they accepted, that is, if they accepted equity or would only cash do.
- What I needed to do to qualify for the loan.

I found out that most, although not all, of them, did strictly traditional lending. After I called and asked all of my questions I would move to the next name.

I spoke to about a dozen lenders before I found one that would listen to my plan. I submitted financial records that were not too appealing, but also a business plan, which I put together myself, that was very sound. They saw what I saw: a no-lose situation where homes that were needed would be built on available land. I also showed where construction money could be saved after seeking answers of experts in building and construction. I secured a loan for $840,000 without putting up any collateral. All I needed to close the deal was a handshake and a smile.

Never having done anything construction-related myself I was at a slight disadvantage, but other people's experience came in mighty handy. My wife worked in the construction industry and we had a mutual friend who was just starting out on his own building homes. I talked to our friend and asked him if he would help me as sort of a consultant. In return I agreed to let him do as much of the actual building as he wanted. It was a match made in heaven. Also, my wife's connections in the industry enabled me to buy a lot of the materials at a very discounted price. It took about six months from the day the idea for building began to churn in my mind to the moment we broke ground.

I started the project in May 2002, quit the post office in July (my wife stayed at her job—she's still there because she enjoys it), and completed the project the following October. All ten units are rented. The land, and the construction, cost about $770,000. I took out $60,000 from the original mortgage of $840,000 to finance other projects. Here's the breakdown:

Cash put into property

Down payment:	$ 0
Closing costs paid by me:	$3,500
Repairs/renovations paid by me:	$0
	$3,500

Monthly cashflow analysis

Rental income:	$7,900

Monthly expenses:

–Taxes (property):	$40
–Insurance:	$200
–Repairs/maintenance:	$0
–Trash collection:	$150
–Reserve:	$100
–Management fee:	0
–Loan payment (25 years at 7%):	$6,100
	$6,590
Net monthly cashflow:	$1,310

Cash-on-cash return

Annual cashflow ($1,310 × 12)	$15,720
÷	
Cash put into property	$ 3,500
Cash-on-cash return	449%

Note: While I don't pay for utilities I do pay for trash collection. However, I raised all the tenants' rates by the amount necessary to cover it. Additionally, two or three tenants have expressed interest in buying a property. If I decide to sell, I would finance 25 percent for them so that I would still be getting my residual income.

While I was in the middle of this project I started building my own house, in another St. Cloud suburb. Much larger than our first house (the new one is 4,800 square feet, more than double the size of the other house); my construction costs came in at about $360,000. I took a $420,000 mortgage at 2.9 percent special financing. In yet another example of how contacts pay off, I approached a mortgage broker I knew who, like me, had left his post office job. By putting 25 percent of the price down, I qualified for the low mortgage rate.

When we closed on the loan I received a credit line of $140,000. This money will be used to either finance more construction and/or buy more rental property to pay for our personal dream house.

This year I'm also planning to build five single-family homes for some of my existing tenants as well as others. I project $600 a month in passive cashflow from these properties. In three years, with additional homes built, I project the income to rise to $2,000 a month. In seven years, the goal is to have enough homes to bring in $4,500 a month plus equity. At that point, with almost $60,000 in passive income, I plan to retire.

Seeing Is Believing

The numbers tell my story. Here's the before-and-after short version as reflected in my financial statements:

Prior to Real Estate

Monthly Bills		*Monthly Income*	
$1,000	mortgage	$2,000	my job
$800	credit cards	$1,550	my wife's job
$400	student loans	$3,550	total
$500	vehicles		
$360	day care		
$1,000	living expenses		
$4,060	total		

Assets		*Liabilities*	
$160,000	real estate	$145,000	house
$14,000	retirement plan	$80,000	credit cards and student loans
$174,000	total	$225,000	

After Real Estate

Monthly Bills		*Monthly Income*	
$1,800	mortgage	$2,150	rental income
$500	credit cards	$1,600	my wife's job
$400	student loans	$3,750	total
$800	vehicles		
$360	day care		
$750	living expenses		
$4,610	total		

Assets		*Liabilities*	
$2,030,000	real estate	$1,370,000	real estate mortgages
$14,000	retirement plan		
		$65,000	credit cards and student loans
$2,044,000	total	$1,435,000	total

No More Dead End

I love to see the goals I taped to the wall over my desk when I bought the triplex: They are:

- In one year, $1,000 in monthly passive income.
- In five years, $5,000 in monthly passive income.

Currently my monthly cashflow is more than twice what I projected. I'd like to share what I've learned:

- Think outside the box. Solutions to problems are in each of us in our own unique way. You don't need someone to always tell you exactly how to solve them. After all, what fun would that be?
- Listen to others. A lot of people who are skilled at what they do love to talk about it. If you just listen you can constantly learn from them.
- Admit that you don't know how to do everything. It's okay. Seeking the help you require will help you achieve success.
- Don't be scared to be rich. I grew up in a house where money was not talked about with the kids, or even among the adults. If you can discuss everything else, why not money?
- Pay attention all the time. When I'm driving past land I'm always thinking, "What can I use that for?"
- Give to receive. Be generous with what you have. Always try to make things work for everyone. For instance, I mentioned that I'm building homes for some of my renters who want their own homes. I'm giving them considerable discounts because I can afford to do so.

Here's the Ticket

When I started my quest to be financially secure I didn't know how good it could feel. I think what Robert Kiyosaki says is true: If you can't see yourself as rich you'll never be able to realize it.

I find it interesting that so many people buy lottery tickets. Sick of their jobs, they long to become rich. But they don't think about what it would be like to be that way without winning the lottery. If you are tired of the rat race

I can tell you that the opportunities to make you wealthy are right outside your door. If I can take advantage of them, you can, too. It's a much more reliable way to make money than depending on a lucky draw. If you allow yourself to believe in yourself and what you're capable of doing, you'll never rely on a lottery ticket again.

Chapter 9

A Mutual Decision

WADE AND CAROL YAMAMOTO
Waikele, Hawaii

We always thought that investing in real estate was far too risky. Buying property meant exposure to uncertainty, which, in turn, could lead to the loss of money. It was too forbidding, too scary for us to consider.

Playing it safe when it came to our retirement investments may have soothed our nerves in the short term because we never lost what we considered to be a lot of money. However, neither did we make a lot of money. And we did sustain a loss of about $20,000 in a work retirement fund when the stock market, and particularly the high-risk stocks in which we were invested, began to slide.

Fear of the unknown, coupled with worry about what others would say about us, was a powerful obstacle. When we heard about *Rich Dad Poor Dad* from a friend in 2000, we were intrigued because Robert Kiyosaki comes from Hawaii originally, as we do. We live in Oahu but I was born and raised on the island of Kauai and Carol comes from the Big Island. We both earned degrees (in electrical engineering and early childhood development respectively) from the University of Hawaii. My parents, who attended trade schools, pressed for a college education for my sister and myself. College was the ideal conveyed to Carol as well. Higher education led to higher income. That's what we were told and that's what we believed.

But reading about someone else's history of success made us skeptical because it's a lot different from actually getting out there and achieving it on one's own.

Yet when we read *Rich Dad Poor Dad* we were struck by the easy, enjoyable manner that Robert Kiyosaki used to put forth his information. We were absorbing so much information about financial independence. At the same time our fear of real estate investing began to disappear. When we began to play the CASHFLOW games with the friend who introduced us to the Rich Dad philosophy something else happened. I began to realize why I didn't want to be dealt either an engineer or a doctor profession card to start the game ("Anything but those!" I moaned more than once). They made getting out of the rat race that much harder. A janitor card, I saw, could help me win the game. Looking at the different occupation cards when we first began playing, we noticed that the higher paid players also had much higher expenses and more doodads. It took them a lot more work to get the passive income to surpass the expenses that are required to get out of the rat race and onto the fast track. Yet, the occupation cards really mimicked real life in that more income meant the bigger house, better cars, and so on.

Playing the games really opened our eyes but until we moved ourselves into the I (investor) quadrant we didn't realize how true the games really were. There's something else we learned: If you keep playing the games but don't apply the knowledge you're getting in your life, you're just wasting your time by not realizing the full power of what you have in front of you. The game offers an incredible education.

Carol had already made a step into the B (business) quadrant several years before. A preschool teacher in a private school, she decided to make a big change to lower her hours by going part-time, as she was getting burned out. I supported her decision. Today, Carol stays at home full-time to run our network marketing business, which we've been doing for the past seven years.

Moving On

By mid-2001 we told ourselves that if wealth was in our future some tough decisions, including significant lifestyle changes, were required. Looking around at the three-bedroom house we lived in (seven years before, when we bought it, we believed that owning a home was the dream of all families), we saw it in a whole different way. We paid $2,000 a month—without utilities—to live there. We bought it for $300,000, and like a lot of people we knew we expected to sell it at some unspecified future date for a lot more money. We put money into renovating the house, and by this time the real estate market for these homes had bottomed out. We couldn't refinance our loan because we had no equity. We hoped the house would appreciate in value but it never did.

But if we sold the house, which was eating up too much of our income, we could begin to play the "game" for real.

Carol's first reaction was, "What will our friends think?" In response, I asked her if she wanted to live there for the next twenty years. Thinking about it, she said no. Then we went through the "what if" list:

• What if we sold the house and used the money to buy real estate that would give us monthly income?
• What if we lived someplace that didn't cost us as much money?
• What if we stayed where we were and did nothing?

We talked over each point at length, which allowed us to figure out what we both wanted to do. "Why are we in this house?" was a question we had to answer honestly.

We sold the house for $260,000, taking a loss, and purchased a townhouse in April 2002. While I must say that moving toward the I quadrant was the biggest, and initially the hardest, thing we'd ever done as a married couple, we didn't regret it for a minute. We felt it was the only way to begin to achieve financial independence.

Three months later we bought our first rental property in Honolulu.

Here's How We Did It

We followed one big tip from Rich Dad's advisor's *Real Estate Riches*: We make money when we buy. We bought our first foreclosure investment for $57,000 with 10 percent down. This first toe-in-the-water investment will give us a return on investment of over 42 percent in the first year. We bought our second foreclosure investment just four months later for $63,000 with 10 percent down. We will receive a return on investment of over 36 percent.

Both properties are three-bedroom, one-bathroom condominiums within a large apartment complex that holds over 100 units. A similar apartment in the building just sold for $83,000.

The two properties, which are about four miles away from where we live, were brought to my attention by my real estate agent, who is also my retired boss. A Navy commander, she became a real estate agent in Hawaii a couple of years before her retirement so that she would have the income to allow her to live there. One year before she became an agent she started buying properties and in three years amassed seven or eight of them. I knew I wanted to learn from her. She was willing to help and share her knowledge.

Before contacting her, we had checked the Internet and newspapers for property but by the time we made contact, the properties were gone. We turned to our agent and explained what we were willing to pay and what return we were seeking. Understanding and encouraging, she pointed out that there are always properties to buy and that we would find the right one at the right time. She was right.

Here's the breakdown of the first rental property, which we purchased in July 2002:

Purchase price: $57,000

Cash put into property

Down payment:	$5,700
Closing costs paid by us:	$1,900
Repairs/renovations paid by us:	$3,500
	$11,100

Monthly cashflow analysis

Rental income:	$1,150
– 5% vacancy loss:	$57.50
Total income:	$1,092.50

Monthly expenses:	
– Taxes (property):	$15.37
– Insurance (PMI, private mortgage insurance):	$53.85
– Repairs/maintenance:	$0

(Everything possible—flooring, appliances, plumbing—was changed in the renovation, so hopefully there won't be repairs for some time.)

– Reserve:	$0
– Monthly maintenance fee	
(includes hazard insurance):	$252.29
– Loan payment (30 years at 7.75%):	$352.15
	$673.66
Net cashflow:	$418.84

Cash-on-cash return

Annual cashflow ($418.84 × 12)	$5,026.08
÷	
Cash put into property	$11,100
Cash-on-cash return	45.3%

Here's the breakdown on the second rental property, which we purchased in November 2002:

Purchase price: $63,100

Cash put into property:

Down payment:	$6,310
Closing costs paid by us:	$2,200
Repairs/renovations paid by us:	$3,500
	$12,010

Monthly cashflow analysis

Rental income:	$1,150
– 5% vacancy loss:	$57.50
Total income:	$1,092.50

Monthly expenses:	
– Taxes (property):	$19.09
– Insurance (PMI, private mortgage insurance):	$42.59
– Repairs/maintenance:	$0

(Everything possible—flooring, appliances, plumbing—was changed in the renovation, so hopefully there won't be repairs for some time.)

– Reserve:	$0
– Maintenance fee (includes hazard insurance):	$252.29
– Loan payment (30 years at 7.875%):	$411.77
	$725.74
Net cashflow:	$366.76

Cash-on-cash return

Annual cashflow ($366.76 × 12)	$4,401.12
÷	
Cash put into property	$12,010
Cash-on-cash return	36.6%

We've learned to *not* fall in love with the properties (although that's not hard to do when they're in foreclosure condition), just with the numbers. In the two cases above, we didn't even see the units until our bids were accepted. We've been fortunate enough to have a real estate agent/mentor that is on the same wavelength as people like Robert Kiyosaki and Dolf de Roos.

By the way, after we closed on the second property, Carol asked, "Why did we take so long to sell our home?" (We chuckle about it now.)

Now we're looking for our third property. With the passive monthly income from that investment, the mortgage payments on our townhouse should be covered. This is an incredible financial turn-around for us.

One Foot Out of the Rat Race

I'm still in the E quadrant, working on a military base where I assist in overseeing a division that monitors the phone system. I'm thirty-nine, and I've already told my boss (he's thirty) that I intend to retire by the time I'm forty-five. That's a big difference from the official minimum retirement age of sixty-two. Within the next three to five years, my goal is to move into the B quadrant with Carol, while we both stay in the I quadrant. At that time our real estate investments and network marketing income should take care of us while we learn about, and seek out, bigger deals. And even though Carol could earn more money in the short term as a teacher, our long-term plans have turned to how we can be in control of our lives. That means not going back to being an employee and using income to buy "stuff" instead of earmarking it for investment.

We Set an Example

Observing what I was doing with real estate, my supervisor also chose to take action for his personal financial life and purchased his first rental property through my real estate agent, who was his former boss also. A friend in

Las Vegas is seeking rentals to buy as well after seeing our results. But other friends don't pay attention to the Rich Dad warning of only doing deals that will spin off cash as soon as they are done. Instead they seek properties with zero cashflow—and even negative cashflow—with the hopes that they will appreciate and can be unloaded at a profit. We tried that strategy with our first single-family home and ended up losing all the capital we put in—and then some.

The only person we trust regarding money is our investment real estate agent. A financial planner, who didn't have a clue about what I was doing, is history. "Do you have positive cashflow rental properties?" is the question Robert Kiyosaki asks, and it's the one we ask potential money advisors, too.

Controlling Your Life Can Happen

When we sold our home, we didn't know whether our lives were spinning out of control or we were taking a step in the right financial direction. When we bought our first rental, we began to feel that we had done the right thing. And anytime we felt ourselves starting to falter we would re-read the Rich Dad books or play the CASHFLOW game again.

When we found our second rental, we knew wholeheartedly that we chose the right direction to go in. It's incredible how one decision can make such an impact.

We always held self-confidence that we could succeed financially. We just didn't know how to do it. It took playing a game for us to understand how to win in life.

Better yet, we overcame the fear of the unknown—what would happen if we sold our house, what would happen if we took a leap of faith in ourselves and invested in real estate. Once we did it we found it wasn't as hard as we thought it would be. While we're nowhere near where we want to be, we're definitely moving in the right direction. It's a far better thing to do it now than be in the awful future position of "If I had only done that back then I wouldn't be where I am now."

Chapter 10

The Power of Three

MERCED HALL
Salt Lake City, Utah

Opportunity came knocking at my dorm-room door during my senior year at Brigham Young University. When I opened the door I saw my friend Aaron, a bit out of breath, so excited and talking so fast that I thought he was speaking Spanish. "You gotta read this, you gotta read this," he insisted, waving a purple book in my face. "It's about this guy who had a rich dad. Well, his real dad was poor, but his rich dad was . . ."

I stared at him blankly, not having a clue about what he was talking about. Knowing Aaron, I wasn't surprised by his display of jittery enthusiasm. It wasn't the first time he'd brought me a book. Grabbing the book from his hand, I promised him I'd look at it and get back to him.

To give myself a break from studying I started reading it. I found myself really wrapped up in the story of Robert and his rich dad. But pressing concerns vied for my attention. At twenty-one, I was studying for midterms and writing papers on my major in management information systems. I was about to earn a degree from the business school and I was busy interviewing for jobs and preparing for graduation. With all those commitments, I put *Rich Dad Poor Dad* aside and eventually returned it to Aaron, who was delighted to get it back.

Generation X Meets "How Did This Happen to Me?"

Right after graduation I landed a dream job at a start-up dot.com. Like my peers, I figured I would make my fortune and retire early by cashing in my incredibly valuable stock options. The idea of working for decades before being able to retire belonged to another generation.

The plan turned out to be a pipe dream that quickly went up in smoke. Three months after being hired I was laid off. The stock options were worthless. Retire young? The belief that could happen plunged with the Nasdaq.

Next I found a job as a software engineer. By this time I knew that I absolutely hated being an employee. Every payday I was reminded why people hated taxes so much. I could not believe that much money was actually cut out of my pay. Before I graduated from college I fantasized about all the stuff I was going to buy when I was working. But between taxes, car payments, and rent, I didn't feel like I was much better off than I was when I was a student. I had worked so hard in school to get into college, and then I worked so hard in college to get accepted into my major. Then I worked so hard keeping up my grades and doing internships so I could mine the golden nugget, that is, "find a good job." *And this was it?* Sitting in a cubicle ninety hours a week staring at computer code on a monitor wasn't exactly my idea of fun, especially since I didn't get to keep most of the money I "made."

Angry and fed up after a couple of months, I remembered Robert and his rich dad. I went home and told my husband, Jeff—we were newly married—about the purple book Aaron nearly forced on me. We decided to go to the bookstore and buy a copy to read together. After that we bought *Rich Dad's CASHFLOW Quadrant* and *Rich Dad's Guide to Investing*.

Jeff is the proverbial entrepreneur. He is great at knowing what people want plus he is an avid negotiator. However, he had grown up being literally taught that "entrepreneur" was a four-syllable four-letter word. In his home, businessmen were considered subhuman and nicknamed "wheeler-dealers." Jeff's dad is a teacher, so he thinks a lot like poor dad did.

So, Jeff did what society expected him to do. He attended the University of Utah, where he earned a bachelor of arts in Japanese and bachelor of science in finance. Getting a really good job was his goal.

Jeff interviewed with several big firms. His grades were near perfect, he had been awarded several scholarships, and he spoke and wrote fluent Japanese. So, he was puzzled when he scored several second and even third interviews but secured no job offers.

Jeff usually handled the rejection pretty well. One particular time, however, he took it very hard. He, along with his identical twin brother, Jon (who happened to have majored in the same subjects and scored the same GPA as his brother), were selected out of 1,000 applicants to go through a meticulous screening process. Both had applied for a financial analyst position with one of the Big Five accounting firms. They were interviewed about half a dozen times, and from the whole university, only Jeff, Jon, and another person were selected to go to the company's headquarters in San Francisco for a final interview. Gossip had it that once you made it that far into the interview process you were in.

Jeff and Jon came back from the trip so nervous and excited that they could barely contain themselves. Finally, the phone call came: Jon was offered a position in the financial/banking division. Jeff wasn't.

I had never seen Jeff so emotionally down. Feeling lost, he kept asking me what he was going do with the rest of his life. He had done everything society told him to do and he felt like a failure. Listening to the well-intentioned advice of others, he decided to go to grad school to study business information systems. That way, he thought, his chances of landing a really good job would improve. He took his GMAT, and was accepted into an excellent school. He would begin classes in the fall of 2001.

But I could not help but wonder if advanced schooling would help us. According to Robert Kiyosaki, more education would probably throw us deeper into debt. We would be digging a hole of liabilities instead of building up assets. Plus, after grad school, Jeff would probably get a corporate job and I hated my corporate job enough for the both of us.

One day I asked Jeff to sit down and listen as I read to him from *Rich Dad's Guide to Investing:*

"'Your first decision is to figure out in which quadrant you have the most chance of achieving long-term financial success.' . . . Pointing to the E quadrant, I said, 'You don't have the expertise that employers will pay the big money for, so you'll probably never make enough money as an employee to invest with. Besides, you're sloppy, you get bored easily, you don't have a very long attention span, you tend to argue, and you don't follow instructions well. Therefore, your chances for financial success in the E quadrant don't look very good.'"

We looked at each other and knew we didn't want to be employees for the rest of our lives. Neither one of us possessed the traits of good workers. Jeff realized that grad school was not for him. Even though I was glad to have gotten a college education, I knew that using it to climb the organizational ladder wasn't for me. Concentrating on who we were and what we yearned for was our goal.

Jeff and I became big Kiyosaki fans. We began to be so touched by rich dad's down-to-earth approach to business and to life that we quoted him. "Rich dad says . . ." became part of our daily vocabulary.

We Make Changes

I quit my job and we lived on our savings as we cut our expenses. We expanded our horizons and decided to go to any seminar that came to town, no matter what it was. We bought (and keep buying) dozens of tapes about sales, finance, personal growth, motivation, and business. Our end goal was clear: to own a business and to retire young and rich. However, like most things in life, it wasn't easy.

We started our first business, which dealt with cashflow. We would match up finance companies with small businesses that needed quick cash. The start-up costs were about $7,000. And while it failed six months later and we lost about $10,000, the learning experience was invaluable.

Unfortunately, we were running out of money.

"You're crazy! You'll never make it, go get a real job!" Our friends and family kept telling us to snap out of the "get-rich-quick scheme" mind-set. It seemed anything but quick.

But we constantly reminded ourselves of two things. Rich dad said failure is part of the process of success. Deepak Chopra said that success is a process, not a destination. That's what kept us going.

Now I was beginning to understand why rich dad told Robert that preparing to be rich requires all the mental preparation that someone climbing Mount Everest needs. Choosing to be rich and following through with it takes everything you've got. You have to want it so badly that you're willing to learn all the hard lessons that come along the way, no matter how difficult they are.

I have to admit that this period was a true test of character for me. My personal obstacles—fear and laziness—would kick in. Sometimes I considered getting a job and forgetting about retiring young and rich. Sometimes I thought I should just become a homemaker and nag Jeff to find a job to support me. After all, I was a woman. I was raised thinking the man is supposed to take care of the bills. Now and then, yearning for some sense of security, I would break down and cry.

In the beginning of our journey I had a very hard time not having a teacher inform me when my assignments were due and when the test was. Sometimes I felt weird without a boss telling me what to do and when to do it. It's funny how I had hated a schedule set for me before, but now that I had none, I was lost. Learning self-discipline was tough.

Jeff announced his thoughts loud and clear.

"If we don't figure out how to start our own business and just get regular jobs, we'll bring in enough income to pay the bills. But then what?" Jeff asked me. "We'll just keep working forever, even when we get old. We're in our twenties. Social Security won't be there to take care of us by the time we reach retirement age. We must figure out how to do what we need to do, while we still have time . . . We can't afford to take the 'easy' way out."

I knew Jeff was right. Sooner or later, figuring out where the money was going to come from when we couldn't, or didn't, want to work anymore was crucial. We were young. We could make a choice.

And we made it. We chose to not be employees. We would rather fail a thousand times than get up every morning for the rest of our lives trapped in the rat race. We stopped wallowing in our failure and moved on, all the while keeping focused on our goal to retire young and rich.

Rich dad said that most millionaires failed three times before they succeeded. We came to the conclusion that figuring out what our next business would be was next on our agenda.

We Try Again

We thought that maybe playing more CASHFLOW 101 would help. It did. After a lot of rounds, we came up with a strategy to get out of the rat race in the game. Our strategy was to first buy a little house with a small amount of passive income. Then, when the right buyer came, we would sell the house and use the cash to buy bigger deals with more passive income. The bigger deals would get us out of the rat race a lot faster than the small deals, but beginning with the small deals was necessary.

We advanced to playing CASHFLOW 202, where we realized that it was possible to buy capital gains deals, liquidate them, and then use the funds to buy cashflow deals. Based on the games, we decided to use our newfound strategy in the real world. We put two pieces together: lump sum of cash + real estate = flip. Our next move was to flip a house but we knew we needed someone else on our team.

We wanted Jon to join us. We knew he was having a challenging time in the corporate world. Disenchanted by corporate politics, he disliked the selfish, promotion-hungry attitudes portrayed in the corporate culture. He realized quickly that he was in the wrong work environment and had to figure a way out.

Before Jon's encounter with corporate America, he had also been reading Kiyosaki. Taking rich dad's advice to heart, he decided not to follow the spending habits of his peers. Despite abundant pressure from his surroundings, he rented a cheap place, didn't buy a car, packed his own lunch, and lived on one third of his income. He was able to save $20,000 in ten months. Jon often reflected back on rich dad's philosophy of "the rich don't work for money" and "don't be addicted to a paycheck" to keep him motivated in his quest to cut his expenses and break free of the rat race. Jon and I often talked about the fact that no matter how high up the ladder we got, we would still be employees with a higher salary.

Reading Kiyosaki, hating his job, and realizing how big of a bite taxes and expenses had on his paycheck, Jon decided to rethink his plan to work at his job for five years. He decided to cut it down to a year and to learn as much as possible during that time. To his surprise and delight, he was laid off after working for ten months.

Jeff and I tried to persuade Jon to join us before and after his layoff. However, he didn't want to move back to Utah. Jon loved living in San Francisco. He decided to start his own import-export business in the Bay Area by partnering up with a friend. However, after a couple of months of market research and cost analysis, he realized his business would not be profitable. Now all of us had failed businesses under our belt. Jon finally gave in to our pleas, and returned to Utah. Our business triumvirate was formed. We were ready to buy real estate.

Here's How We Did It

We looked at hundreds of houses and analyzed them to figure out what deal to buy. Dolf de Roos, Rich Dad's advisor and author of *Real Estate Riches*, says that his ratio of structures that he looks at versus structures he makes offers on versus amount of offers accepted is 100:10:1. That was the case with us. We scoured the Utah market for weeks but didn't find any deals that fit our parameters. The deals we did find were being taken up by cash offers.

So we looked harder. We analyzed, negotiated, made offers, talked to dozens of real estate agents. Sure enough, Jeff found our first deal, an old grandma two-room bungalow with potential that reeked with the hideous smell of cat pee. It was dark and in need of a new kitchen, roof, and bathroom. Some people even suggested that we bulldoze it. It was priced at $75,000. When we offered $40,000, the agent freaked out. If we hadn't known from Dolf de Roos that real estate agents are required by law to present all offers to the seller, I would have thought that she wasn't even going to pass it on. So, despite the odds, we wrote up the offer anyway. Finally, after weeks of deliberation, the seller decided to take $45,000 for the property. However, the terms of the offer were cash at closing, and settlement within seven days of acceptance of the offer.

We became totally desperate. By this time we barely had enough in our bank account to keep us fed. Considering the circumstances, it was ironic that we were so excited over a cash offer acceptance.

We tried bringing in a partner that could come up with the money (he would fix up the house after it was bought), but he got too greedy and tried to take the house from under us. "How can I trust you? You're too young," was his parting shot after offering $46,000 for the house.

By the time all this happened, we only had three days left to come up with a counteroffer of $50,000. We brainstormed and pulled all-nighters and figured out a way that we could come up with the cash. We discovered that we could transfer advances from our credit cards directly into our bank accounts. Instead of a cash advance rate of 19 percent, we'd be getting the 0 percent transfer promotional offer for six months. We did it. We put Jeff's, Jon's, and my credit cards together and raised the cash. The property was ours.

(Let me stop here and make something clear. I know that rich dad warns against using credit cards frivolously. We were very careful when we decided to do this, and we examined meticulously the financial risks associated with this decision. I would not recommend this strategy to anyone who doesn't have the experience or financial literacy to make a decision based on this kind of a risk-reward ratio basis.)

We bought the house for $50,000 and then put $15,000 worth of renovations into it. The house was appraised for $115,000 and we sold it three months later for $113,500. After paying off our credit card debt we kept the net profit as our seed capital. However, according to rich dad, "buy and flip" properties are not a goal to strive for, since positive cashflow is the aim of a property owner. So we were dealers, not investors. However, rich dad also says that "buy and flip" opportunities can help build cash reserves for eventual investment in cashflowing properties. And that's what we did.

We used some of that seed capital to put a down payment on another house in Salt Lake City that we rented out. We got a really good deal on this particular property, which we bought for $159,900. Average monthly rents in the neighborhood, which was in the yuppie side of town, were between $1,200 and $1,600. Since we fixed it up to prime condition, we were able to sign a two-year lease for $1,580.

Here's the breakdown on this single-family home (3,200 square feet with six bedrooms and four baths):

Cash put into property

Down payment:	$7,995
Closing costs paid by us:	$7,150
Repairs paid by us:	$4,500
	$19,645

Monthly cashflow analysis

Rental income:	$1,600
−Vacancy loss (5%):	$80
Total income:	$1,520

Monthly expenses:	
—Taxes (property) and insurance:	$161
—Repairs/maintenance:	$0

(Per contract, tenant responsible for repair costs, and the tenant takes care of expenses for trash collection and yard work.)

—Reserve	$20
—Management fee (10% of rents):	$160
—Loan payment (30 years at 5.8%):	$960
	$1,301
Net monthly cashflow:	$219

Cash-on-cash return

Annual cashflow ($219 × 12)	$2,628
÷	
Amount of cash put into property	$19,645
Cash-on-cash return	13.4%

Today the property is appraised at $210,000.

What We're Doing Now

Our current strategy is to flip lower-end houses and to buy and hold mid-end houses like the one mentioned above. We have figured out that in our particular market, we are able to buy lower-end houses at a discount, fix them and sell them at premium. Plus, the smaller houses we can now buy for cash, so all the financing costs that would be taking money off of our bottom line are eliminated. We then proceed to sell the lower-end houses in the less-affluent part of town to people who can't find decent affordable housing.

Because the lower-end houses do not spin off as much positive cashflow as mid-end houses do, we take each one on a case-by-case basis. We run financials on each property—the prices vary from $50,000 to $150,000—and based on the numbers we decide whether to sell or to hold. At this point we have purchased nine single-family homes, sold five, and kept four.

We get more money out of our properties than the rent market value because we market them very well. Plus we make sure that the homes really look good so we end up renting to tenants who are willing to pay more—we average about 10 percent more than the going rate. Factor in that we buy our investments below market value and you can see that we win on either side of the ownership equation.

We also screen our tenants, checking their credit rating, references, and employment history thoroughly.

Here are the numbers for a duplex (2,500 total square feet with six bedrooms and three bathrooms) we just acquired:

Purchase price: $70,000

Cash put into property

Down payment:	$ 7,000
Closing costs paid by us (seller paid):	$0
Repairs paid by us:	$35,000
	$42,000

Monthly cashflow analysis

Rental income:	$1,825
—Vacancy loss (5%):	$91.25
Total income:	$1,733.75

Monthly expenses:	
—Taxes (property) and insurance:	$208.30
—Repairs/maintenance (6% of rental income):	$109.50
—Reserve:	$50
—Yard work:	$20
—Management fee (10% of rents):	$182.50
—Loan payment (30 years at 7%):	$419.14
	$989.44
Net monthly cashflow:	$744.31

Cash-on-cash return

Annual cashflow ($744.31 × 12)	$8,931.72
÷	
Amount of cash put into property	$42,000
Cash-on-cash return	21.27%

Today the property is appraised at $164,500.

We are in the process of refinancing this property so we can get the cash back that we put in for repairs and the down payment. By refinancing and increasing our loan amount, our monthly mortgage payment will go up to $698.57, which will make our net cashflow decrease by almost $280.

However, we will still have a positive cashflow of $650 per month and have $42,000 to put toward our next investment property.

Here's the breakdown on another duplex (2,300 total square feet with five bedrooms and two baths):

Purchase price: $97,000

Cash put into property

Down payment:	$9,700
Closing costs paid by us:	$2,910
Repairs paid by us:	$18,000
	$30,610

Monthly cashflow analysis

Rental income:	$1,600
–Vacancy loss (5%):	$80
Total income:	$1,520

Monthly expenses:	
–Taxes (property) and insurance:	$192
–Repairs/maintenance:	$96
–Reserve:	$50
–Yard work:	$25
–Management fee (10% of rents):	$160
–Loan payment (30 years at 7%):	$580.81
	$1,103.81
Net monthly cashflow:	$416.19

Cash-on-cash return

Annual cashflow ($416.19 × 12)	$4,994.28
÷	
Amount of cash put into property	$30,610
Cash-on-cash return:	16.32%

Today this house is appraised at $159,000.

As far as the houses we flip go, we buy them for all cash at 50 percent to 60 percent of market value. Mostly we buy homes with cosmetic issues and no structural problems. We sell them for nothing down and we pay the closing costs. They are fully financed by the bank, so we carry no second mortgages. When we sell them we are completely done with them.

The breakdowns for homes that we flipped are different from the rentals. This is the breakdown on a single-family residence (840 square feet with two bedrooms and one bathroom) that we flipped:

Purchase price:	$48,000
Down payment:	$48,000
Closing costs (seller paid closing costs, in this case the bank):	$0
Repairs:	$250

(This house was a foreclosure of an investor who had fixed it up but went bankrupt before he could sell it. Everything—from the carpet to the kitchen cabinets—was new and immaculate.)

Monthly expenses:	n/a
Taxes (property) and insurance:	n/a
Management fee:	n/a
Loan payment:	n/a
Rental income:	n/a
Monthly expenses: included in repair costs:	
Net cashflow:	n/a
Equity:	$48,250
Appraised value:	$95,000
Cash-on-cash return:	n/a
Total appreciation:	$47,000

We sold this house for $94,300. Our buyer got a grant from the city to pay for her closing costs, so we didn't pay for them.

Our total costs:	**$48,250**
Sales price:	$94,300
–total costs:	$48,250
Net profit/capital gain	$46,050

Before and After

We began to buy houses in the beginning of April 2002. Here's where we were financially before we bought our first property:

Expenses			Income	
*Civic	$400		Mom's help:	$250
Credit cards	$253			
**COBRA	$285			
**Medical	$100			
*Cell phone	$80			
Rent	$400			

Fixed Expenses	
*Food	$300
*Gas	$100
*Other	$200
Expenses:	$2,118
−income	250
Total expenses	($1,868)

*Tax deduction
**Partial tax deduction

Assets			Liabilities	
Checking:	Merced	$230	Car loan	$6,397
	Jeff	$524	Credit cards	$12,478
Total		$754	Cell phone	$240
				$19,115
Savings:	Merced	$440	−total assets	$1,274
	Jeff	$80		($17,841)
Total		$520		
Total assets		$1,274		

January 2003 Balance Sheet

Assets		Liabilities	
Savings	$65,000	Credit cards	$1,500

Portfolio			
Stocks	2,700	Car Loans	25,000
Trading account	18,500	School loans	0
Real estate	890,500	Mortgages	324,000
Assets subtotal	$976,700		

Doodads

Cars	$36,000
Jewelry	12,000
Other	15,000
Doodads subtotal	$63,000

Total assets according to banker (Assets subtotal + doodads)	$1,039,700
Total assets according to Rich Dad (Assets subtotal only, not adding doodads)	$976,700
Total liabilities	$350,500
Net worth according to banker (Total assets according to banker less total liabilities)	$689,200
Net worth according to Rich Dad (Total assets according to Rich Dad less total liabilities)	$626,200

January 2003 Income Statement

Monthly earned income

Self-employed mortgage broker	$10,000
Flipping houses (average income per month)	$17,500

Monthly passive income

Real estate (net)	2,900

Monthly portfolio income

Monthly trading premiums	2,000
Total monthly income	$32,400

Monthly expenses:	
Taxes	$4,860
Credit card payments	150
Rent	500
Car payment	800
Food and clothing	500
Insurance	500
Cell phone	200
–Total Expenses	$7,510
Net monthly cashflow	$24,890

Where We Are Now

We are still in the transitional period between the left and the right side of the cashflow quadrant. The fact that we flip houses puts us in the S quadrant (since at this point we're very personally involved in the process). We are currently working on a business model to transition our flips into a B. However, the fact that we lease out some of our properties makes us Bs, because we are getting passive income.

All three of us are very involved in what we do. I decided to also follow rich dad's advice of "the rich don't work for money" and figured that since our core business was real estate, I should learn as much as possible about mortgages. I've become an independent licensed mortgage broker who does deals with different banks. I'm really enjoying it, and I'm learning a lot that I know will help our business. Amazingly enough, I have started making decent money doing mortgages and I certainly don't mind the extra cashflow. I don't plan on being a loan officer forever, just long enough to hire the best mortgage advisor I can find. Being as knowledgeable as possible is just plain smart.

Kiyosaki says to never fall in love with an investment vehicle. So, even though real estate is what we have started doing, we do not want to limit ourselves. We want to become involved in business ventures of all kinds, as long as the numbers make sense.

Our goal is to buy and hold big real estate deals like apartment complexes and commercial buildings, not just in the United States, but also internationally. Since Jeff and Jon are fluent in speaking, reading, and writing Japanese, we would like to do some business with Japan. Jon also speaks Thai, so Thailand is also on our list. Both Jeff and Jon can read Chinese characters and they want to expand our business there (especially since China has such a huge potential for business). Jeff and I speak Spanish, so we also want to be involved in business ventures in Latin America.

I started applying Kiyosaki's principles in my life when I was twenty-four. I am twenty-five right now. Jeff and Jon were both twenty-eight, and as you can probably guess, they're twenty-nine now. We started out with no assets on our balance sheet, only liabilities. Our income statement had more outflows than inflows. Those outflows were mostly doodads. Our only source of income was earned income.

In a year, we have bought over $1.25 million worth of real estate, and we have kept $890,000 of it. Now we have passive income, portfolio income, and earned income. We are trying to follow Robert and Kim's goal (when they first got started) of only spending 70 percent of our income and putting aside 10 percent for investing, 10 percent for savings, and 10 percent for charity. We don't really spend on doodads anymore. We're being frugal while we build our business, but once we have hit rich dad's definition of rich, we know we won't have to be so frugal anymore. We're still defining what retirement means to us, but I figure that in five years we'll know what it is.

Take the Time You Need

Although anybody can do what we have done, it took us a year just to get into the right frame of mind before we even bought our first house. It also took a lot of emotional preparation, and a lot of education. We are still always learning. It might take other people less time to prepare than it took us, or might take them more time. It depends on the person.

But, regardless of how long it takes someone to prepare, we want to emphasize the fact that preparation (i.e., learning about real estate at a macro level, as well as at a micro level, and becoming skilled in investment and financing strategies) takes time and effort. It takes a lot of patience, too, as well as a lot of self-control, especially over emotions. That's why we're such big rich dad fans. He lays out each emotion that investors need to overcome.

In real estate, we regard fear as the most crucial emotion to overcome. People become afraid they will never find a good real estate deal, and then go and buy a bad one because they are afraid if they don't buy now, they will never buy. We say no deal is better than a bad deal. We have also seen landlords get so afraid that they will never get a tenant that they rent to the first person that drops by (maybe that's where all the landlord nightmare stories emanate from).

It's better to lose a couple of months of rent finding the right tenant than renting to a tenant that will trash the property and never pay rent.

We also see people who become so afraid that something will go wrong with the house they are buying that they forgo a fabulous deal. They don't take the necessary steps to inspect the house or work with the numbers so that they can hedge potential losses.

While we aim to inspire others in their quest for success at the same time we want to evoke a sense of caution. Basically we don't think people should expect that they are going to make it big in real estate overnight. There are a lot of "investors" around us who have gone broke trying to rent or flip a house. We actually bought a foreclosed home from one of these "investors."

That's why being prepared is so important. We made sure to acquire experience in real estate before we got ready to buy. We did it by putting in offers although we couldn't buy the property, by reading a lot of books and checking Web sites, and by researching our local market. Also, we talked to a lot of real estate agents, brokers, and investors and got a lot of useful information that way. Real estate isn't complicated to do when you know what you're doing and the process is ongoing. We still learn every day.

In our opinion the two keys to real estate success are to get control of your emotions and to keep an open mind because you will be learning every day.

Gen-X Alert

Jeff, Jon, and I know a lot of people our age whose lives were thrown into a tailspin when the dot.coms crashed. A lot of dreams were shattered and feelings of security were replaced by fears about the future. If this happened to you, as it did to us, here's the most important thing to remember: *Don't let fear stop you from attaining what you think is lost.*

Facing fear every day means managing it. You can beat disappointment by holding on to that dream and attaining it in a new way. Think about what you want, really listen to yourself, and then do it. Along the way, surround yourself with like-minded people who will support you and not try to sell you something that doesn't work, like 401(k)s. The biggest risk is doing nothing.

If it wasn't for Robert Kiyosaki and his advisors, Jeff would probably still be in grad school, and Jon and I would be working in the corporate world and hating it. We are so very grateful to have been pointed in the right direction! We know we still have much more to learn, and that we still have many failures to confront before we reach our ultimate goal. But we're excited and we look forward to it. Thanks, rich dad!

Chapter 11

Change of Mind

KEN HOBSON
Philadelphia, Pennsylvania

My vacation plans were simple: decompress on the pink sands of a Bermuda beach with my wife, Sue. It was 1999, I was tired, and the last thing I wanted to do was focus on anything. Not even a book.

As it happened, Sue had asked some friends to recommend reading material for our trip. *Rich Dad Poor Dad* was one of them. She bought a copy and tucked it in her bag. When our flight was delayed I caved in and opened the book. I read it at the gate. I read it on the plane. When Sue begged me to accompany her to those glorious beaches, I said she'd have to wait until I finished the chapter I was riveted to. After I finished reading the whole book, I started it over again.

How could I not, when the thrill of recognition ran up my spine? "That's me!" I thought when Robert wrote that lack of planning was the route to failure. That was *my* problem.

I felt sure that there was another way to secure the financial future for my family but I couldn't figure out what it was. Yet the clues were all around me. When I was a boy and my family would drive from New Jersey to Brooklyn to visit relatives, I'd see signs advertising property for lease and wonder why. Now the answer was clear. Leasing meant money flowing in to the owner of the property, month after month. I thought about neighbors who owned a day care center. Every two years they leased a new car. Suddenly I understood: The car was a business expense. So were lots of groceries. "Duh—that's what they're doing!" I exclaimed as I literally smacked myself on the side of my head. Things began to click because I was ready to comprehend them.

As soon as we got home I bought other Rich Dad books, tapes, and games. I was a sponge for this new and welcome information.

The Past Is Prelude

When I was growing up I never knew there was more than one way to think about money. Having lived through difficult economic times, both of my parents craved financial security. They found it by working for the state of New Jersey and the federal government for thirty-five years. Today they live off pensions.

My parents were consummate level one investors. Income-producing investments were—and still are—alien to them. I call this a classic World War II mentality. One time, when I was about nine years old, we fell very far into debt. I remember watching my father remove mail from the box and instead of taking it inside the house stuff the bills down beside the car seat. With the heat shut off, my brother and I, trying to get warm, hunkered down in our sleeping bags at night. He and I knew there were problems but they weren't discussed.

Those tough times left me with the empty, defeated feeling that only a handful of ways existed to achieve financial stability. I could either: a) work decades toward earning a pension, b) save money, or c) marry rich. How I could eventually teach my own children to reach this goal in other ways was never addressed.

So I looked at my options and figured that the computer industry was the most potentially lucrative career path. Other than an aunt who became a biologist, I was the first person in my extended family to go to college.

My job history included trading up positions every couple of years to something better. By the time *Rich Dad Poor Dad* captured my attention, I was working as a project manager and Internet programmer for QVC, the hugely popular and successful Internet and television shopping network. While I liked my job, and I earned a very good salary, something was missing. I believed that Sue and I were set as long as I kept working until I was fifty-nine and a half, when I could tap into my 401(k), our big investment. (There was an additional $6,000 that we had sunk into the stock market.) That meant twenty-two years to go.

But I didn't want to *have* to work until I was almost sixty. I sensed that there just had to be a better, smarter way to be financially secure. Like a riddle tickling my brain, I tried to find the solution to scratch that itch. Sue and I had both graduated with degrees in computer science from Rochester Institute of Technology. With all our combined education and experience—Sue found success selling payroll services—the answer kept evading us. That is, until I found what I was looking for.

Instead of a one-way road to questionable financial security that I was supposed to follow because no other routes were open to me, I was going to chart a new course to financial freedom. The Rich Dad map showed me that opportunities flourished all around me.

The First Step

For two years I applied the lessons I was learning. We took out the $6,000 in the stock market plus another $10,000 from an IRA termination, to invest in real estate. (A stockbroker neighbor thought I was out of my mind to do this. However, the money I pulled out is alive and well and living in real estate equity. If I had let it sit in the stock market I would have lost one third of the money. The stocks were a roller coaster, a thrilling ride on the way up and a stomach churner on the way down.)

Most of the properties I bought were purchased with stock profits prior to the stock market crash in mid-2000. I've found that real estate is the safest investment.

Here's How I Did It

The first thing I did was research. I joined an investors group that featured Investing 101 classes for rookies like me. I paid about $60 for a weekend class, and this was money well spent. I received an overview of investing along with what to know about repair work. This included walk-throughs where the class saw before and after houses. Information about how much each repair job cost was covered: flooring, plumbing, roofing, drywall, and so on. The classes were invaluable—they gave the participants a solid grounding about educated guesses where total costs were concerned.

- The next step was a business plan. I identified the amount of positive cashflow I wanted, which was a target of a minimum of $150 a month per property after taxes.
- Then I looked for a working territory, preferably not more than a half hour away, in which to search for properties.
- After I did that I checked rents to see the range of prices for properties similar to the ones I was interested in.
- From there I researched mortgage quotes and a rough estimate of taxes for the area. I also asked about association fees, insurance costs, and water and sewer bills.
- I totaled up all the costs incurred to own the property I was after, and that number was my base cost. I discovered that my potential properties required $700 to pay all costs, which meant that I had to determine if the market would support rents between $850 and $900 a monthly.
- I began to search for properties valued between $50,000 and $70,000, which allowed a mortgage between $400 and $500 a month.

Those properties were foreclosures. I went to the HUD and VA sites on the Internet to get a list. (I did find a better list, which indicates all foreclosure proceedings, existed on the docket at the county courthouse.)

I purchased three foreclosed properties, all single-family homes in Pennsylvania, with equity in our home, along with money from stock sales. (I know that a lot of people use equity to pay off debt, or to buy a boat or some other nonasset. We paid down much of our debt so that our line of credit was almost fully available. Controlling debt means freeing up leverage.) All the deals I've done to date have been with about 10 percent down of the asking price.

Here's the breakdown on a couple of those houses:

Purchase price: $89,000

Cash put into property

Down payment:	$9,000
Closing costs paid by me:	$1,800
Repairs/renovations paid by me:	$3,500
	$14,300

Monthly cashflow analysis

Rental income:	$1,075
Monthly expenses:	
—Taxes (property) and insurance:	$325
—Repairs and maintenance:	$0
—Reserve:	$0
—Management fee:	$0
—Loan payment (30 years at 8%):	$575
	$900
Net monthly cashflow:	$175

Cash-on-cash return

Annual cashflow ($175 × 12)	$2,100
÷	
Amount of cash put into property	$14,300
Cash-on-cash return	14.6%

Today the property is appraised at $123,000.

Purchase price: $120,000

Cash put into property:

Down payment:	$12,000
Closing costs paid by me:	$2,400
Repairs/renovations paid by me:	$1,200
	$15,600

Monthly cashflow analysis:

Rental income:	$1,450
Monthly expenses:	
—Taxes (property) and insurance:	$432
—Repairs and maintenance:	$0

—Reserve:	$0
—Management fee:	$0
—Loan payment (30 years at 8%):	$807
	$1,239
Net monthly cashflow:	$211

Cash-on-cash return

Annual cashflow ($211 × 12)	$2,532
÷	
Amount of cash put into property	$15,600
Cash-on-cash return	16.2%

Today the property is appraised at $156,000

To be honest, I made mistakes, too. Not adhering to the business plan was the problem. One property, another single-family home, which required a drive of several hours to reach, was a real fixer-upper. The kitchen was usable—if you kept your eyes closed—then you wouldn't see the rust coating the metal cabinets. I thought I'd buy it for $40,000 and sell it for $60,000. However, this fantasy scenario had little to do with reality because I ignored the market. I should have turned it around quickly for $45,000, but I didn't.

One year later, the kitchen was still an eyesore and I still owned the house. I spent three months and $5,000 fixing up the kitchen and bathroom and eventually I sold it for $72,000. However, because I held on to the house for so long I paid a lot of money in real estate taxes and ended up only breaking even.

But real estate is very forgiving; it always gives you another chance.

A New Way to Work

In the fall of 2001 I gave notice that I was leaving QVC to make a major career change. Because of the confidence I had gained buying properties, I began working for the largest investment real estate brokerage firm in the country. Today I broker multimillion-dollar properties to individuals and partnerships. The interesting thing is that although I lacked a background in selling, I was hired because of my knowledge of the investment market as well as the goals and mind-set of the investor.

Frankly, everyone I knew, with the exception of Sue, thought I was crazy. How could I leave such a secure job to work for myself—at real estate, no less? It was tough trying to explain that the job no longer held any excitement for me. After all, one computer screen is pretty much the same as the next.

But, the naysayers pointed out, I had dabbled in my own businesses before, and they didn't work out. Their unshakable belief was that the stock market was the means to achieve financial security.

I didn't see things that way. The past businesses didn't succeed because they were jobs. I did start an ISP (Internet service provider) in 1998 and it's true that it went belly-up because the business systems weren't in place. Basically, I moonlit as a computer programmer, so I was self-employed, not a business owner.

But I don't want to give the impression that no sweat was involved in this big change. The day I began I was ready to sell. It didn't happen that day. Or the next. Or for the next three months, either. Doubt started to creep in, and the mantra, "What did I do? I haven't seen a paycheck in months," began to repeat itself in my brain. I reached for the phone, ready to call QVC, where I had an open invitation to return.

Then I remembered Robert's words: Analyze, don't criticize. Don't second-guess yourself. Taking a deep breath along with a reality check, I told myself to hold on for a second. The company that hired me was solid. Opportunities were still out there. I had my own track record to remind me that I knew what I was doing. Sue and I didn't make a snap decision that I should take this job. We discussed the pros and cons and agreed that it was the right move to make.

Sure enough, things began to change after that. I just completed a deal that will pay me more than I made in 2001 at QVC. Four more deals are lined up behind it and more are in the works, including a twelve-unit apartment with laundromat. I am on pace to quadruple my income within eighteen months of going into my new career.

Life Is What You Make It

Our children, who are nine and five years old, are learning to manage money because we discuss how to do so with them. Players of CASHFLOW for Kids, they know about the destructive pull of the doodad.

We also play CASHFLOW 101 regularly with friends who are not in my business. There's a lot of talk about fears about jobs and money and some people don't want to take what they still perceive of as a risk.

My old view was that a 401(k) was a low-risk investment because it was diversified. My new view is that if a deal doesn't immediately make money then it's risky. No clear exit strategy is risky, too.

Three years from now I plan to be on the fast track with cumulative passive monthly cashflow of $5,000. But even now I enjoy enormous freedom. I pick my hours. I decide when to stay home with my children, when to golf and fish, and when to show a property. This lifestyle can't be beat. Still, after I retire I will continue to do real estate brokerage because I love helping others achieve financial freedom.

I've learned so much in the last several years, and my education continues. For me, the basics are to be:

- Committed to my decisions.
- Aware that the path I'm taking is well traveled.
- Humble. I can always learn more—and I don't have all the answers.
- Confident about what I am doing. I've found that everything comes together when I resolve that I can do it.
- Patient. My immediate timeline may not be realistic, but eventually I'll get where I want to go.
- Ready to plan my work and work my plan.

There is another factor that I want to express. I knew what I was doing in my old job because that's what I was trained to do. But I still lacked self-confidence in my ability to change my financial future.

The day I gave notice I knew I was embarking on an adventure. I would never have made the leap without the confidence in the knowledge I gained and the awareness that I could use it to my advantage. Considering that laziness was the obstacle I had to overcome (sometimes I still have to kick myself in the butt to get going), I'm in an amazing place. But then again, it's the place I want to be.

I know that there are millions of professionals who drag themselves back and forth to work every day because they need to pay the bills. They aren't where they want to be. But there is a way to that place. It exists. I found it. So can you.

Part IV

Never Too Young to Achieve Financial Success

I believe that all kids are born rich kids and smart kids. All the young peo-ple in this section who sent their stories to me—a ten-year-old girl living in Alabama, a thirteen-year-old boy in California, and two college juniors in Indiana who happen to be best friends—are proof that it's never too early to begin a financial education. Although Allison, Jake, David, and Michael are at different points in their lives, they have something in common: Each one is finding his or her way toward financial freedom by making choices about how to live and how to earn passive income.

Instead of feeling entitled to having money just handed to them, they are setting goals, achieving them, and creating income on their own. Still in school, they are learning to take control of their lives.

Like me, they had teachers who helped them understand that getting a financial education never begins too early. Parents and an innovative high school teacher provided the information that showed them that cashflow possibilities exist at any age. Allison listened to her mother's Choose to Be Rich *tapes in the car and had an idea for a moneymaking business. Jake watched his parents invest in real estate using the Rich Dad information, and understood that there was no reason he couldn't do it, too. David and Michael, working toward their college degrees, not only applied a financial education to their own lives, but made it available to others as well. Playing the CASHFLOW game in high school altered the way they looked at how they wanted to live, earn money, and impact their society. They took that expanded view with them to college where they are applying it as well.*

No one sat down with any of these young people and forced them to come up with a plan to make money. None of their parents threatened to stop their allowance. Instead, the group was inspired by the Rich Dad information and created successful ventures on their own.

Allison, Jake, David, and Michael received a head start on the road to financial security by grasping what was available to them and then taking the next steps. They demonstrate that age does not matter when either starting a business or buying real estate as an investment. Without hesitation— and without fear—*they figured out what they wanted to do and then did it. Unlike many adults, they haven't been told year after year about what they can't or shouldn't do. Not being afraid to try and possibly fail has brought them success to build on. They didn't let anything or anyone stop them from accomplishing their goals.*

All of them exhibit an entrepreneurial spirit willing to face challenges and take risks. To achieve their goals they are sharpening their financial skills, boosting their entrepreneurial spirits, and having fun in the process. Already they understand the difference between earning a salary working for someone else and building assets to give themselves financial security. Once they read, or listened to, or played with Rich Dad information, they knew that opportunities beckoned and they were better able to recognize them. They have an "I want to succeed" mentality.

Allison, Jake, David, and Michael are continuing to learn that:

• *Allowances and gifts of money can be turned into assets that will make money.*

- *Investing in one's future means investing right now. Immediate gratification is not as rewarding as future cashflow.*
- *Even though they are students, they live in the real world. They know about finances, assets, liabilities, and what they need to do to become financially secure.*
- *Setting an example for others, and teaching them what they have learned, is an important part of life.*
- *Debt is nothing to be afraid of if it is good debt. They understand that borrowing to acquire an asset is good debt and is a wise course because assets bring income. It is your money working for you.*
- *Giving back is one of the most important aspects of being rich.*

They are a terrific sampling of the next generation of people who are already learning how to rely on themselves for financial security, a powerful Rich Dad lesson that everyone needs to know. Beginning so early, investing time and effort to earn cashflow is becoming natural for them. As you'll see, they already know that all kinds of possibilities exist for them.

Energetic, thoughtful, and winning, they are an inspiration to anyone who has ever thought, "I wish I had the courage to do that." Their enthusiasm and "I can do that!" outlook is contagious. Read on and be inspired.

Chapter 12

Never Too Early

ALLISON KUBALA
Cumming, Georgia

Last year, my fourth-grade teacher asked my class to write a report about someone who inspired us. First I picked my mom and then I picked someone who no one else in my class thought of: Robert Kiyosaki. I know a lot about what he says because my mom plays his *Choose to Be Rich* and *Rich Dad Poor Dad* tapes in our car when she drives me and my younger brother to school, the mall, or other places.

She also bought the CASHFLOW for Kids game. My whole family played, including my brother, Eric, who once became a millionaire before I did. He was seven at the time. Now he's eight.

Listening to the tapes got me thinking about making money in a different way. My $5 a week allowance, and sitting at the corner selling lemonade after school on weekends and in the summertime, just wasn't getting me enough money.

My mom keeps teaching my brother and me to save our money to buy the things we want. A lot of times we would be in stores and I'd see something I really, really wanted and asked to borrow from my allowance. And she always said, "No."

I wanted extra money to spend. To make that happen I decided to start my own business. I was nine. I learn a lot in school, but from the Rich Dad tapes and the game I saw that it's possible to start your own business no matter how young you are.

First I sold rocks to the neighbors for aquariums and decoration. My mom thought it would never work but I went door-to-door and I did make some money. And like Robert's rich dad and my mom told me, I kept track of what I spent and what I earned.

Then I decided to sell candles. I made some for my third-grade Christmas party and liked doing them. I learned something new along with being responsible for buying the stuff I needed to make them.

First I tried selling them door-to-door and on the street, but I wasn't very successful. Then I decided to sell them on the Web, where age doesn't matter at all because nobody ever saw me.

I became a business owner. My mom helped me set up a Web site. I made up business cards and handed them out at school and at church. I bought what I needed by saving my allowance. As soon as I received an order I made the candles and shipped them out.

My start-up costs were between $20 and $30. So far I've made between $50 and $60. I'm doing so well that I now have an assistant—my brother, Eric.

I feel like I can accomplish a lot more by listening to what rich dad says. Finding my own way to do things isn't hard. I know I can take something I like to do, turn it into a business, and make it work. I also understand that if I put my mind to something I can accomplish it no matter what happens. I even got all As on my report card!

Chapter 13

Playing a Winning Game

JAKE COLMAN
Venice, California

I just bought my first rental property, a single family home in Florida. Brand-new, it contains three bedrooms and two bathrooms. In and of itself, that might not sound so unusual. However, I'm thirteen and a half years old. To me, investing in real estate makes sense. When I tell you how I came to this conclusion, I think you'll agree with me.

Just a Few Years Ago

"I want to play, too!" I announced to my parents when I saw them playing a new board game about three and a half years ago. The game board reminded me of Monopoly, which I liked but found a little easy after a while. This game looked like fun—and it had an interesting name.

Playing CASHFLOW 101 was entertaining but at the same time I found myself learning about a lot of things that I didn't know existed. I also felt myself being drawn to the information, which was kind of surprising. I didn't expect details about what a good investment property looked like and how to read a balance sheet to appeal to me. The game showed me the difference between an asset and a liability and how to analyze the numbers in an investment. It wasn't hard to learn and the math was pretty simple. I just hadn't seen numbers applied in that way before.

Best of all, I saw that there was another approach to money that I hadn't considered previously. Sure, I liked to spend money, but the idea of acquiring it the way the game suggested was so new to me. Before the game I thought property meant the house you lived in. Now I understood why there were "for lease" signs on buildings. People who owned the buildings wanted to rent space for money. Real estate had value.

But real estate wasn't the only investment I learned about. Understanding the difference between a stock and a mutual fund was a basic piece of information that came in handy. The game convinced me that in order to make money in the stock market you must know what you are doing.

After we played the game my parents and I would talk about what did and didn't work and why. The first time I played, it took me a couple of hours to get out of the rat race. A couple of years ago we started playing CASH-FLOW 202, which is the advanced version of CASHFLOW 101. Now I can get out of the rat race in less than thirty minutes. The great thing about the games is that they gave me the facts I needed to know before making a move. I began to see that I could apply the rules of the game to real life. When you know what you're doing, risks get a lot smaller. There's a lot less fear involved about going forward with your plans.

You're Never Too Young to Invest in Yourself

When I was about six or seven years old I opened a lemonade stand in front of our house, which is located across the street from a church. My business soon became a hit with the hot and thirsty people streaming out of church after Sunday services that were held four times that day.

By reinvesting my profits into the business, I bought a small shaved ice machine and began offering flavored ice along with the lemonade. On hot summer days, people would be lined up around the block to buy from me. I was sold out almost every week. Soon I was able to buy my first computer with the profits. (To do that I added money I earned by helping my dad in his business as well as washing cars and doing jobs around the house.)

My folks always supported me in my businesses and they've helped me learn about material cost versus selling price, how labor costs affect profit (like the times my friends helped me at the lemonade stand and I paid them), and the importance of good marketing and promotion.

In the fifth grade I started making custom candles. That year in school, candle making was an elective. I discovered that I liked to create candles. Even better, I discovered that people liked to buy them.

One day, my parents and I were eating in a popular local restaurant when I noticed that every table held a candle. I saw an opportunity and I asked the owner how I could help supply him with candles. We struck a deal for a monthly bulk order.

I borrowed about $500 from my mom to get started. I had to figure out whether making the candles by hand would be cost-effective. Trying to determine how many I could make before school, after school, and on weekends was part of the process. When I saw that making the candles myself wouldn't be the best way to go, I did some research on the Internet and located a candle supply company. Not only did I find a good source of finished candles, I found better supplies for my custom-made candles, too. Whew!

Knowing a steady supply of finished candles was available, I went to other restaurants and talked to the owners. I offered them incentives like free delivery. And yes, they listened to me and believed in my ability to fulfill my commitment, despite my age. I didn't disappoint them. Even when an unexpected glitch came my way, I didn't panic. Once, after I placed my order, a restaurant cut back on the number of candles. But I didn't sweat it because candles don't spoil. I was able to use the extras to fill another order.

Recently I took my kit to our synagogue's Hanukkah celebration, which was also a fund-raiser, and invited kids to make their own candles. They loved it. I sold to their parents all the custom-made theme candles I brought with me, and I donated a portion of what I received back to the synagogue. I know how important giving back is.

One year after receiving her loan I repaid my mom. The business brings in a profit of about $1,000 a year. My dad set me up with an accounting program on my computer so that I could keep track of my business and I show him regular financial statements so we can know how I'm doing. I mentioned to my dad that I would like his bookkeeper to go through my books to make sure that my financials are accurate.

My most recent business venture was designing a graphic advertisement for my dad's company. That was a very instructive episode. I spent eight hours working on the piece and I earned really good money. My salary was more than the candle business generates in a year. But when I received my paycheck I couldn't believe how much money went to taxes and how little was my own. Even at my age, I knew there was something wrong with that.

That's why I'm glad my parents, along with Rich Dad, are teaching me about becoming financially independent so I won't have to depend on a weekly paycheck. After watching my parents buy real estate over the past couple of years, I told them I wanted to buy a rental property of my own so that I could be prepared for college and start to become financially independent.

Here's How I Did It

The first thing I made sure of was that the numbers worked.

The purchase price was $111,600 with 5 percent down. The down payment came from my own savings, including bar mitzvah gifts, and profits from my businesses. Because this is a brand-new house, I don't anticipate that any major maintenance or repairs will be needed for a few years. There is a ten-year new home warranty to cover any major expenses. Any future maintenance or repairs will come out of accumulated surplus in the house account. Here's the breakdown:

Cash put into property

Down payment:	$5,580
Closing costs paid by me:	$1,520
Repairs/renovations paid by me:	$0
	$7,100

Monthly cashflow analysis

Rental income:	$1,125
— Vacancy loss (strong rental market in Florida):	$0
Total income:	$1,125

Monthly expenses:	
— Taxes (property) and insurance:	$350
— Repairs/maintenance:	$0
— Reserve (cashflow will help to cover my expenses):	$25

— Management fee (5% of rent):	$56.25
— Loan payment (30 years at 6.5%):	$670
	$1,101.25
Net monthly cashflow:	$23.75

Cash-on-cash return

Annual cashflow ($23.75 × 12)	$285
÷	
Amount of cash put into property	$7,100
Cash-on-cash return	4%

Okay, I know this doesn't sound like a lot, but this first property is similar to the first property my parents bought. (Actually, I'm doing better, because that rental initially had a negative cashflow.) I see this purchase as a way to build cashflow while the tenant pays the mortgage. And while the cash-on-cash return is just 4 percent (excluding appreciation and tax advantages), my money is working for me and my property has potential for appreciation. The developer is now selling the same home for $126,000. That's over $14,000 more than I paid for my house.

If the house appreciates in the next two years as I anticipate, I can have the private mortgage insurance (PMI) removed, which will increase the cashflow. Private mortgage insurance is additional insurance required by the lender on certain properties.

And over time I can raise the rent, which will produce more monthly cashflow as well. The passive cashflow I'll receive every month will help to take care of my expenses while I concentrate on school. Worrying about money won't eat into my time. If the house appreciates enough, I can refinance the mortgage and pull out cash to use for college expenses (another option would be to take this money and buy another property). I just don't see a downside to this kind of investment.

My folks secured the loan for me, since I have no credit history or income (not enough to qualify for a mortgage anyway). But my name is on the deed, along with my parents' names. All the rental income will go into a separate account of my own and all expenses will be paid out of this account. If any repairs or maintenance are necessary the money will be taken from the positive cashflow.

Rich Dad taught me to invest in assets instead of buying doodads. And that's exactly what I'm doing.

I'm Just Beginning

Another really important lesson I am learning is how to structure deals so that everyone wins. I want to build a personal submarine, which measures approximately ten feet by three feet and carries two people, in order to raise the awareness of the current state of our oceans and the need to preserve our marine wildlife. I will need approximately $25,000. In order to get the funding for this venture I am looking for companies to sponsor me. In exchange for their funding or donations, I would give them advertising space on the bright yellow sub.

In this way the company will get valuable advertising and good publicity, and I will get to build the submarine. That is a great way to structure deals because no one walks away unhappy.

My mom and dad stress that education is an important part of a person's life, but it isn't the basis for financial security. By learning how to invest wisely and manage my money now I'm starting to build a solid financial future. And although I left the lemonade stand a while ago, the candle business is still ongoing and I intend to keep it running. By the time I enter college I can hire people to run it for me.

It's never too early to start becoming financially independent.

Chapter 14

We Want to H.E.L.P.

David Hosei and Michael Slate
Junior Year, Indiana University,
Junior Year, Purdue University

Going to college is as much a privilege as an opportunity to find out what a person wants to do with his life. We view our university years as an integral part of shaping our interests as well as providing the grounding we need in our chosen fields. But we also received a pre-college education that served us before we ever left high school. Both of us were kid entrepreneurs. Now one of us plans to create businesses after graduation. The other one already owns real estate. We're normal guys who were incredibly fortunate. We had a teacher who changed our financial lives. We met him in high school.

Let's Back Up a Bit

We met in elementary school and, growing up in Indianapolis, we played plenty of games together. Monopoly was a particular favorite because we could buy lots of real estate properties and railroads and utility companies with money that was magically provided without any effort on our part.

How money really worked in the world remained pretty much a mystery until our senior year in high school. That's when we took a class called Marketing Co-op, which was taught by Mr. Dave Stephens.

Sitting in that classroom, we received the kind of lessons students really need. Mr. Stephens gave us the necessary skills to succeed in life. How to interview for a job was part of the lesson plan. So was building entrepreneurial skills. Then we learned how to invest in real estate. (We were seventeen years old and the idea had *never* occurred to us before. We were aware of investing in real estate, we just didn't understand the fundamentals. After all, how could a student afford to buy property? Little did we know.) The time value of money was another part of the curriculum. For example, $1.00 today will not buy as much as $1.00 did in 1960. We also learned that the timing of an investment was important, but not the most important part, and that simply investing money in sound ventures was a great way of building financial wealth. We were encouraged to learn at our own pace. Books were suggested and *Rich Dad Poor Dad* was on the reading list.

One day Mr. Stephens brought a board game into class. By that point, we weren't surprised. We just wondered how it would apply to the focus of the class. The next three classes were devoted to playing this game, CASH-FLOW 101. We really enjoyed it; it was fun. And yes, we learned a lot, too. The game showed us how to get out of the rat race as well as how to use money to buy sound investments. Getting a job after college and working for years at it was the path we were on. Still, we knew that we were different and wanted another lifestyle. The game gave us a structured picture of that lifestyle and explained why we were different. The compelling aspect about the game was that it provided a visual reality to accumulating passive cashflow.

Then someone mentioned that there was a CASHFLOW for Kids game and suddenly an idea took hold. Another person mentioned knowing a fifth-grade teacher at a local elementary school. Why not teach kids even younger than we were the skills they needed? Why wait until high school?

Arrangements were made and a group of us went over to the fifth-grade class. We figured that introducing what the game was about in a fun way was the way to go. So we put on a skit, including such memorable numbers as "The Grinch That Stole Cashflow."

The kids loved playing the game. And those ten- and eleven-year-olds were savvy. When we heard them say things like, "My passive income has to be more than my expenses in order for me to get out of the rat race," more than a few of us felt goose bumps. We knew that the game was giving these kids a whole new way of looking at life—not just money. Very likely they were learning lessons their own parents had never been taught. Certainly that's what our experience was.

After we graduated from high school, a few of us decided that teaching college students about finance could provide quite a ripple effect. Those students could, in turn, teach kids about money. And they could do it in a way that was fun. This was a stepping-off point for us, the beginning of our quest to help educate others in our communities about financial literacy, entrepreneurship, and money management.

Lending a Hand

To do that we began a nonprofit organization called H.E.L.P., Inc., which stands for Helping Educate Lots of People. The organization employs CASH-FLOW for Kids to teach local children near college communities about money management, financial literacy, and entrepreneurship. To make that happen, we do outreach programs at the Boys and Girls Clubs, Girls, Inc., elementary schools, the Indiana Department of Education Conference, national conferences, and high schools.

Chapters of the organization are in place at Purdue University, Indiana University, and Wabash University. Ball State University and IUPUI (Indiana University and Purdue University of Indianapolis) are next. So far over 100 college students have reached over 200 ten-, eleven-, and twelve-year-olds a year. We've found a really efficient way to make this happen. Ten dedicated college students meet once a month to learn the game. They teach other college students, who, in turn, reach out to children in the community. It's a simple formula: Learn. Teach. Do.

How we arrived at this juncture reveals a lot about opportunities that exist for young entrepreneurs who want to build on what they instinctively know. We want others to gain access to the information that was made available to us. Once they have it they, too, will possess a terrific advantage for succeeding in life. Our stories will probably be familiar to lots of people—millions of teenagers possess an entrepreneurial spirit. But unlike them, we got a helping hand that we want to pass on to others.

DAVID: ENTREPRENEUR AT TWELVE, BUSINESS SELLER AT SEVENTEEN

Growing up I always looked for business opportunities. By the time I was twelve, I collected aluminum cans for recycling while my friends played basketball. By fifteen I worked as a busboy on Friday and Saturday nights at my grandmother's country club. (I still work shifts there when I go home during breaks.)

The spring of that year a friend, who had his own lawn mower, and I formed a lawn care service. The decision was easy. All around our neighborhoods there were lawns, and a lot of people who owned homes either weren't interested, or didn't have the time, to take care of them. We figured we could. To make the businesses work, I needed two things: a lawn mower, and the money to buy it. I went to my sister, explained what I wanted to do, how much I could charge, and how many lawns we could tend over a weekend and after school. I also promised to repay her within two months.

Convinced that I knew what I was doing, she lent me $500, interest free. I was able to repay the money in one month (but I continually repay my sister in favors because I could not have gotten where I am today without her help).

To expand our market, we told teachers at the high school about our service. Someone referred us to a bed-and-breakfast, and we worked for them, too. Then we branched off again, and were hired by landlords, home owners, and commercial entities.

Of course, there was one rather significant logistical problem. At fifteen, I was too young to drive, and I had to hire friends to drive me from job to job. I bought the truck and hired my friends to drive it for four months. But as soon as I received my license I drove the truck myself.

By my senior year in high school six friends worked for us. I paid them on the fifth and twentieth of the month on a per-hour basis. The business grossed $40,000 over those years. I made one third of that in profit for myself, another one third of the revenue went toward overhead expenses, and the remaining one third went toward labor. (Three months into the business my partner quit. He did not want to be a part of the business anymore. Over the next couple of years, he really was upset at the decision that he made to quit the business.)

I started looking for prospects to buy my business at the beginning of my freshman year at college. Three months into my college career, I could not satisfy the customers' demands, so they all began to look for new service providers.

I was going to sell the business to a landlord, the biggest client, for $200 a month for five years. But by the time we came to an agreement, I had no customer list to sell. So, I ended up selling the equipment and truck for $1,500 cash.

This experience taught me the importance of using a qualified advisor to mediate during the selling process. As a matter of fact, I learned to use advisors whenever I was unknowledgeable about a specific business process or procedure.

I also learned that a business can die in a period of three months if there is not a sufficient plan in place that will continue offering superior service to customers. I learned that the Rich Dad philosophy can work, but it is challenging and requires a lot of work, effort, and planning.

The profit from the lawn care business came in really handy because while my parents stressed the value of getting a good education on my siblings and me they were also clear about who was responsible for paying for it. My share of the profits from the business, as well as the sale price, paid for my first year of college.

Another Kind of College Experience

Subsequently, I started other businesses. I knew that a business could generate substantial passive income if set up correctly. Some were successful, while some were not. All were meaningful because they taught me a lot. They were:

• A snow removal business, which grossed a little over $3,000 in two seasons. This business complemented my lawn care business in high school. I purchased the equipment the winter of my junior year in high school. I was the co-owner of the business with a high school friend.

• A house painting business, which brought in $2,000 one summer. I did all the work myself.

• A network marketing distributorship, which cost me about $300 along with seventy-five hours of my time. I received training and worked for others in the business, but I found it difficult to persuade friends and family members to become involved. I just wasn't comfortable. But it was an important episode because I realized that finding my own formula and vision and running with them was imperative.

• A computer-related start-up venture, with two others, which required about 500 hours of time but none of my own money. We had entered a business competition, based on our venture, which gave us $5,000 to work with. We offered a way to link medical information using a PC tablet, that is, a screen without a keyboard. One of the team left and the project couldn't move forward. This, too, was an important learning experience because it taught me about trusting people I do business with, especially where money, effort, and time are concerned.

I consider H.E.L.P. a business as well because I am accountable for it and to it.

My expanding entrepreneurial ability helps in other ways, too. I raised $7,500 to showcase a Battle of the Bands competition, which contributed $2,000 to Jill's House, a fund for a student with breast cancer. Over the past two years I've helped to generate donations of over $4,000 to Jill's House.

In addition to starting businesses, I've also invested about $5,000 in stocks. At this point, I'm leaving them alone. Dealing with money every day, however, is something I'm still working on.

Credit Cards Don't Earn Credits

I never thought about budgeting my expenses. Until I qualified for credit cards I used cash. When I finally put credit cards in my wallet I kept thinking that they served several purposes. They allowed me to keep track of my expenses, they were a convenient substitute for cash, and they were so easy to use. But at the time I was focused on paying my bills, not budgeting my money. While I've never paid a penny in interest charges I did see a big spike in how much I spent on food, clothing, and entertainment. This habit of overspending remains my personal obstacle, but giving up would not solve any problems. Continuously working to grow, develop, mature, and learn to overcome my obstacles is my personal mission. I currently pay for everything with cash, debit cards, and online banking.

I'm still straightening out my values. Without a second thought I put down a 15 percent or 20 percent tip for a waitperson, but I still search for the cheapest financial services I can find.

Distractions still vie for my attention. It's funny, because they're the same ones that I had at eleven. "Come out and play," is a siren call. But I look at them as a challenge. Sure, it's important to decompress but it's also necessary to achieve goals.

I See Another Kind of Future

Since I'm still in college, my immediate goal is to graduate with a degree in entrepreneurship and finance. Before I took Mr. Stephens's class I didn't know what I wanted to do. Now I know the direction I intend to go in.

My one-year goal is to start a business and begin to build a financial empire. My five-year goal is to be able to make the decision whether or not I want to retire at that time. Without a doubt, I don't want an eight-to-six, five-day-a-week desk job that does not give me an opportunity to pursue my dreams, visions, and goals. I shudder to think about existing in a real-life rendition of the movie *Office Space*.

Meanwhile, I embrace the chance to teach about money and risk taking because these subjects aren't taught in school. With useful information, young people can enter the door to the world of entrepreneurs instead of being locked out. Currently, I'm a residential assistant in my dorm on an outdoor adventure floor (in return for room and board). Part of my responsibility is to mentor the fifty college students, most of whom are freshmen, living there. Answering all kinds of questions about campus life, future careers, and student activities is part of my job. So is teaching leadership and entrepreneurial skills.

When I was seventeen I felt in control of my life for the first time. I realized that I wanted to be an entrepreneur, to create businesses and live a life that I fashioned for myself, not one I tried to fit into. I'll tell you, it felt great! Maintaining control is both a responsibility and a challenge. Once goals are achieved new ones must take their place. Convincing people that a twenty-year-old has credibility is not easy. But the effort is worth the rewards.

I used to swim in an ocean of ideas. Now I know how to build a boat to steer toward those ideas. That's the information I want to share with every person who thinks about possibilities but doesn't know how to make them happen. For every young man and woman who feels they are different from the mainstream, not destined to be chained to a desk all day, there is more than hope. There's a way to achieve your dreams and your freedom.

MICHAEL: CANDY MAN, PROPERTY OWNER

From 1989 until 1991 I ran the Slate Candy Store out of the entryway to our home. Seeing a need, I filled it. Kids like candy, but the only place to buy it locally was at the convenient mart, and a lot of parents wouldn't allow their kids to go there. It was too far away and getting there required going along a main road instead of through neighborhoods.

I asked my mom if I could sell candy and she agreed. We went to Sam's Club and she bought all kinds of stuff (I knew what my friends and I liked so picking it out was easy). Once I told the kids at school what I was doing, word spread quickly. Soon kids were lining up outside our house. My formula was simple: I doubled the price of each piece of candy and I made a couple of hundred dollars a month after paying for the candy until I gave up the business after a year. My house was robbed and my mom and I decided to quit selling candy.

By the time I was sixteen I transitioned to the digital age. I invested $1,000 (a gift from my grandmother) in my first computer. With an Internet connection and AOL account, I set up a bunch of Web sites where companies paid me, based on a per-click basis, to advertise their banners. Eventually the sites were getting 2,000 hits a day and I was raking in $800 a week. I made several thousand dollars in about four months before the system was changed.

Now I will admit that in this pre–Mr. Stephens time, I blew all my money on a car, a stereo system for the car, entertainment, girls—the basic teenage list. But when I attended his class, I took all my ideas about being an entrepreneur and glued them together. Finally, I understood how it was possible to become financially independent. Money wasn't just to earn and spend.

The information I received not only pointed me in the investment direction I wanted to go toward, it helped to crystallize my goals. I knew that after I graduated from college I would use the next five years to create passive income that would exceed my expenses (like a mortgage, car payments, food, and so on). My ten-year goal would be the *ability* to retire—not that I plan to do so.

To make that happen, I've already begun to invest in real estate.

Here's How I Did It

After living in a dorm room during my freshman year, I decided to rent my first apartment with a roommate. We split the $800 a month rent and tried to settle into the odd layout of the apartment, which, strange as it sounds, was shaped like a wedge of pie. After the excitement of actually being in the apartment wore off, I realized that I was paying $400 a month toward the owner's mortgage payment. I knew there was a better way.

I began studying the real estate market in the area (Lafayette, Indiana) and recognized that it was a perfect time to buy. Interest rates were very low and everyone in the area seemed to be selling at one time. A true buyer's market was set out like a buffet.

Every day I spent a little time searching for a duplex, thinking that I would live in one unit and rent out the other. But after eight months spent looking at forty or so duplexes, I was getting discouraged. Most were built before 1950 and required a lot of time, which I didn't have, for maintenance and upkeep. One day I saw an ad in the paper for a fully managed four-plex with "excellent returns."

When I saw it, I was very impressed. Not only was it less than five years old, it was better than most of the apartments in town. Fireplaces graced each unit, which also contained washers and dryers. The units on the top floors were topped with vaulted ceilings. I could live there in luxury. When the owner presented me with a copy of the financials, an Excel spreadsheet, as soon as I arrived to look at the property, I was even more impressed.

The seller was asking for $245,000, and while he agreed to $240,000, I knew that I should have the property appraised. Sure enough, the appraisal price was $266,000. My research told me that due to economic conditions, most banks only required about 10 percent down. I used the appraisal price as leverage. Here's how that particular bank looked at the numbers. They regarded $266,000 as the price, and 10 percent of it—$26,000—as a cash down payment. The $26,000 existed on paper only.

But then something else came to my attention. By putting 10 percent down I was required to pay for private mortgage insurance (PMI), which is additional insurance required by the bank to help them sell the loan to another bank. The $120 monthly PMI insurance fee seemed like money flushed away. Determined to avoid this payment, I figured out a way to put 20 percent down. I talked the seller into carrying a second mortgage of 10 percent. He agreed and the private mortgage insurance disappeared.

Seeking the best terms, I talked to about five banks over the course of a month. All the people I dealt with were courteous but one, more than the others, was willing to do whatever it took to get me the loan. I presented them all with mounds of financial statements and paperwork, but this person was willing to support me—I was twenty at the time—and work every step of the way to secure the loan. In my case, that included special approvals from the underwriter because of my income constraints. The loan came through, a five-year ARM (adjustable rate mortgage) at 6.375 percent. This means for five years the interest rate is 6.375 percent. After five years the rate can up go or down depending on the current market. I would pay $1,300 a month. (Although I would have preferred a thirty-year loan, which would have locked in a low interest rate for the entire term of the loan, this was the only mortgage I could get. If the rate goes up after five years I may decide to refinance the loan.)

I called my friend David Hosei to help me analyze the financials. If I lived in one of the units I would have to pay about $200 to break even. Here's how we figured it:

$1,300	went to the first mortgage
$189	went to the second mortgage
$262	went to taxes
$1,751	for mortgage payments and taxes

Expenses included:
Management fee: $108 (6% of $1,800 with me living in one unit for $200/month)
Lawn mowing or snow plowing fees, which varied
Insurance (property): about $50
Minor electric fees

Rental income: $1,800

$1,751	for mortgage payments and taxes
+$200	expenses (management fee, $108 + insurance and additional expenses, $92)
$1,951	(plus or minus $100 depending on how much snow we get)
−$1,800	rents
$151	My out-of-pocket costs, less than what I paid for rent.

For $151 per month I could live in a luxurious apartment *and* own the building. It was a go.

After securing the loan, I was informed that closing costs were about $6,000, which meant about $2,000 out of my pocket, plus the one point due to the bank, a number that represented 1 percent of the loan, or $2,600. The amazing thing is this: When I got to the closing I only had to pay $625. It seems that the seller was responsible for more taxes than the lender had originally quoted to him.

My mortgage payment didn't start until the month after I closed on the property. This gave me $1,800 from rents to deposit in my bank account. I am saving this amount in case of emergency repairs and to cover the months when units may be vacant.

After I graduate I will move out and rent that top unit for $625. At that point my passive monthly cashflow will be $440. Here's the breakdown:

$595	for bottom apartment + $25 water + pet money (if applicable)*
$595	for bottom apartment + $25 water + pet money (if applicable)
$625	for top apartment + $25 water + pet money (if applicable)
$625	for top apartment + $25 water + pet money (if applicable)
$2,540	rents (management fee, 6% of this number = $152.40)
−$2,100	mortgages, expenses, plus or minus $100 depending on how much snow we get
$440	monthly passive cashflow

The charge for pets is $25 a month. Tenants pay an initial $200 deposit if they own a pet; $100 is nonrefundable.

Cash-on-cash return

Annual cashflow ($440 × 12)	$5,280
÷	
Amount of cash put into property	$625
Cash-on-cash return:	845%

As far as the property appreciating, investment properties are appraised based upon the amount of income they generate. Therefore if the rent goes up, then most likely the property value will go up, too. I know the property will appreciate because a small shopping center is being built right across the street. Location always counts, whether you're selling candy or selling real estate.

I look at the investment this way. I only put $625 of my own money into this deal, which gives me a terrific place to live and potential passive cashflow. Presently, based upon the appraisal, I have $26,000 worth of equity; by the time I graduate that amount may increase. I plan to use some of this to buy more property.

There is another aspect to this purchase, which I think is important to bring up. I heard a whole lot of critical comments from friends and relatives about investing in real estate at the age of twenty-one. Several people made a point of telling me that I would be fixing leaky toilets and dealing with unbearable tenants. When would I study my major, computer science, much less anything else?

The reality is that the property is fully managed by a trustworthy company. Everything from renting the units to dealing with tenant issues (like nonpayment of rent and complaints) to mowing the lawn is their responsibility. While the management company doesn't pay for services like lawn care, they do supervise them and make sure that everything looks great. All I do is open financial statements every month. I don't even have to go to the bank because my check is deposited directly into my account.

Investing Isn't Just for "Seniors"

Buying the property turned out to be an excellent investment for me—a junior year college student. Without the financial education I received I would still be like most of my fellow students, paying an exorbitant rent with nothing to show for it. While a lot of my peers spend any extra money they get on clothes or a new car, I would rather purchase an investment that generates perpetual income. Some of that income, in turn, can be used to buy what I want, or to generate even more passive income.

Another lesson I've learned is about risk. To me, risk is not starting your own business or investing in real estate. It's relying on the government to pay Social Security benefits forty years from now. Risk is working for forty years, being laid off, and holding on to a worthless 401(k).

Still, I continue to face my own obstacle, which is the fear that some opportunities are just gimmicks. But I'm learning to "analyze instead of criticize." This makes all the difference.

But I have developed another good habit. Every day I take ten minutes to track all my expenses and income. I always know how much money I have and where it is. Ten percent of every dollar I earn is deposited into a special investment account. Another 10 percent goes to charity. Currently I work at Circuit City on the weekends and I run a Web-hosting company, which has 140 clients and is growing steadily.

DAVID AND MICHAEL: WE'RE STILL LEARNING EVERY DAY

In addition to going to school and earning our degrees, we are also working toward our goals of financial independence. We constantly look for and analyze opportunities by scanning the classified ads and by listening to things our peers talk about.

The financial information we were taught put what we were doing, as well as what we could do, in perspective. It gave us a vision of how life can be. Every day we wake up with the amazing feeling of being in control. We feel rich right now. Most of all, this is the experience we want to share with others.

We know lots of people who aren't realizing their potential because they're afraid to do anything other than their "subject." To them, and to everyone else, we want to say this: Do not be afraid. Go after your dreams. Believe us, there's nothing else like it.

Part V

A New Way to Do Business

My rich dad taught me that getting a financial education is important for everyone. For people who deal in monetary matters like tax consulting, financial planning, and running their own businesses, sharing the power of financial literacy is especially important.

Often, men and women whose work involves advice about dealing with personal finances tell me how the Rich Dad information has changed their point of view about their own financial future, as well as how they deal with their clients. It's not as if these professionals weren't paying attention to their businesses. They put in long hours and concentrated on doing the best they could for their clients. They dealt with finances as they had been taught but they weren't getting the returns they wanted. Where their own financial futures were concerned, the same problem existed.

When they started educating their clients with the Rich Dad information, their clients started taking control of their financial lives and the client/advisor roles became stronger and more profitable.

With Rich Dad, their perspectives about money matters shifted. By re-

educating themselves to think like rich people, they not only altered how they did business to give their clients better financial positions, they altered how they handled their personal finances as well. While many professionals fear that educating their clients may mean losing them, these professionals can clearly demonstrate that by educating their clients not only has their relationship improved, these clients are more likely to become long-term clients because their advisor invested time in them through education—not just their money.

In this section you'll meet Tom Wheelwright, an experienced accountant in Arizona who is affiliated with Diane Kennedy, one of the Rich Dad's advisors. You'll read how Tom and his partner, Ann Mathis, approached financial matters so that their clients and their employees could secure strong financial futures. They also applied the Rich Dad information to their own lives by making investments in assets they hadn't considered before and expanding their business in new ways.

You'll also read Brian Eagleheart's story. Like me, Brian is a Marine Corps veteran (as I write this he is involved in the war in Iraq). A financial consultant living in Oregon who floundered with a significant amount of debt, Brian used the Rich Dad books to teach himself a new way to plan finances. He not only helped his clients to get on the road to financial freedom, he reduced his personal debt and increased his monthly cashflow as well as his donations to charity. He took control of his financial life, which fueled his independence. His story is so compelling he told it in one of the Rich Dad infomercials.

People who run their own businesses send us stories about taking financial control, too. In this section you'll meet Michelle LaBrosse, a successful business owner in Connecticut who revamped the way she ran her company based on Rich Dad books and tapes. The lessons she learned and applied had to do with basics that a lot of people tend to ignore. Rich Dad talked often about how important it is to pay oneself before paying bills. In Michelle's case doing so made an enormous difference in how her business functioned and grew.

Terri Bowersock is another successful business owner. Based in Arizona, Terri built her local furnishings business into a nationwide multimillion-dollar company. Her success, combined with her personal story of overcoming a learning disability, earned her coverage by a number of national magazines and appearances on national television shows. Still, Rich Dad presented Terri with new possibilities for wealth that she hadn't known about. Her story is a terrific example of understanding that new opportunities are always available—no matter how successful a person already is.

If you are either a financial consultant or a business owner who wants to see improved results, as well as build personal wealth, take good note of what Tom, Brian, Michelle, and Terri have to say. By teaching others financial literacy, they strengthened their own financial future as well as that of their clients and their businesses. Their Rich Dad experiences are terrific examples of financial successes that continue to grow.

Chapter 15

Accounting for Ourselves

TOM WHEELWRIGHT
WHEELWRIGHT MATHIS PLC
DK Advisors™
Tempe, Arizona

First of all, my partner, Ann Mathis, and I want everyone to know that we are outside accountants for the Rich Dad company. So saying we are gung ho about the information available to us might sound obvious. But it's not. Even with our financial educations and backgrounds—we both earned master's degrees in taxation and there is a lot of experience between us—we found a new perspective about money and investing since we've become involved with the Rich Dad folks. The change has been profound, for us, our employees, and for our clients.

Ann and I became business partners about two years ago but even before we joined forces we were looking for a way to teach financial literacy to our clients. Separately and then together, we felt that the more people knew, the better we could serve them.

As it happened, Diane Kennedy, one of the Rich Dad's advisors, was looking for assistance for her ongoing clients so that she could concentrate on marketing her book, *Loopholes of the Rich*. At the same time we were seeking some help in marketing our tax and accounting service. Before Diane met with us she asked us to read *Rich Dad Poor Dad.* Immediately, we took a liking to the Rich Dad philosophy. After Diane invited us to play CASHFLOW 101 with her, we were hooked.

Ann and I found that as we played the game together, we became better business partners. We were always in tune with one another, but using the language of Rich Dad provided us with an even more efficient way to exchange ideas and information for investing and forming other strategic business plans. Confronting "risks" in a safe environment, using pretend money, and the foresight to know how things can turn out, makes risk management a lot easier. Using the deal cards, which show how to evaluate risks over and over again, makes it less frightening to take a chance. Very soon it's possible to look at a card, assess where potential jeopardy lurks, and decide what to do. It's an extremely freeing mental exercise.

Consequently, making good decisions quickly and efficiently became our norm. At times, people expressed amazement at how effortlessly we decided to expand our business. While we were never averse to taking risks, we found that we were able to evaluate them better. The effect on our business has been profound. We've doubled the number of our employees in the last year because our business continues to grow.

Our employees play the game with us on a regular basis. All of them, including several that are not highly paid, are now real estate investors, a possibility they had not previously considered. Some teach the game. Ann and I wholeheartedly embrace the Rich Dad work philosophy: Go to a job because you love it, not because you need the check.

We also play the game with our clients every month. Actually, we insist that the first step to financial planning is playing the game even if doing so sounds silly to them. We tell them that participating will expand their outlook on finances more than anything else they can do. Our view is that the game is an excellent tool that teaches accounting principles, tax strategies, general investing, and financial management. Our clients, who find the game very instructive, love it.

The first time they play, their strategy often mirrors their own investment outlook. But by the second or third time they take part, they see alternative ways to invest. This moves them to transform the way they look at money and investments. There's another maybe even more powerful benefit. Time and again, those couples who play the game together report back that their personal relationships have grown stronger.

Our clients trust us with their money and we love being able to give back to them a way to expand their financial horizons. The positive changes we see in their lives inspire us to keep doing more for them.

The ripple effect doesn't stop there. Recently we invited one of our stock-broker friends to play with us. Watching him, it seemed apparent that he was unhappy with the results he was getting. By the look on his face when he was leaving, we were concerned that we would never see him again.

Just over a month later, he called to report that he had just closed on his first property and attributed this investment to playing the game with us.

We've observed similar changes when we play the game with parents, siblings, spouses, and children. Sam Wheelwright, thirteen years old, plays the game with family and friends. Frequently he talks about acquiring properties in the future and not becoming an employee. A natural at doing deals, he says that he is learning what he excels at and implementing that talent will help him become rich in the future.

Over and over again we've seen that kids get out of the rat race faster than their parents do because they're not afraid to try something new. Fresh minds not worn down by cynicism and worry grasp opportunities in record time.

We May Be Accountants but We're Investors, Too

While neither of us experienced particular money problems in the past, at the same time we were not making any serious progress toward our financial freedom. We were stuck in the S (self-employed) quadrant.

Now things are different. We are in the process of shifting from being self-employed to building an accounting business that will provide us with a large amount of capital. We plan to invest that money, which will allow us to receive income from our core business without full-time management efforts on our part. Among the many things we learned is that investing is a team sport. A great team of advisors, from attorneys to bankers to real estate brokers, work with us to help achieve our goals.

Our team, which includes Diane Kennedy, allows us to focus on building our business and not trying to be everything to everybody. As accountants we focus on taxes and financial planning. We are not insurance agents, stock-brokers, or personal bankers.

We have also been fortunate in finding outstanding employees who can handle a lot of responsibility and truly care about our business and our clients.

Getting our money to work for us reflects a big change in our investment view, both professionally and personally. As a result of the additional financial education we've received, we've eliminated the 401(k) in our office. These investments, along with mutual funds, were the financial plans we used to rely on. Now we know that far better long-range financial strategies are available.

In the past several months, Ann and I invested in the development of oil and gas wells and we are now working on acquiring multifamily homes as well as a commercial property. This was all new to us. Last year none of these kinds of investments were ours.

In the process of investing and teaching our clients, we learned the magic of real estate. We discovered the enormous leverage of using other people's money that real estate provides. We find ourselves illustrating this to clients every day, showing them how much faster their money can grow in even an average real estate investment than it can in any other type of investment. And on top of that, real estate can provide tremendous leverage for tax deductions. Not only do you get a deduction for your money, you also get a deduction for the OPM (other people's money) you use. It really is magic!

We've also confronted the problem so many people complain about: not enough time to concentrate on personal finances because work takes up so much attention. With the proper team and outlook, we follow our investments because our team of advisors makes it easy for us.

Our goals for the next five to ten years include building our business from being an accounting firm into a national business advisory company that will efficiently assist thousands of people with their daily financial decisions.

For us, the greatest aspect of employing the Rich Dad information is the ability to bring financial literacy to the average person, so that he or she does not have to rely on the tired philosophies of financial institutions and their inadequate investments.

We Built on a Solid Foundation

Ann and I are both fortunate in that our parents taught us that anything is possible. When I was growing up, my dad was an entrepreneur. Along with his brother, he owned a successful printing business with fifty employees. My mom was the controller. My siblings worked in the production department. I, of course, found a place in the accounting department. But there was more; my parents owned rental properties. From an early age I understood the power of business.

But I didn't fully link the concepts I believed to be true with the ability to bring them to pass myself, much less teach them, until my financial education expanded. When I played the CASHFLOW game for the first time and I got out of the rat race, I understood what I was capable of doing. A veteran of working for big accounting firms, I was in my forties. It was time for me to take control of my business and my life.

When I'm asked for advice, my reply is consistent. Become informed. Ask questions. Do what is best for you. And focus on what you want, not what you need. The rest will follow.

Chapter 16

A New Strategy

BRIAN EAGLEHEART
Portland, Oregon

By the time I was twenty-two I teetered at the edge of a financial precipice. One big blast of wind, and I would be blown over into a deep money pit that I'd never be able to climb out of.

A whopping $60,000 in debt, a staggering combination of college (I graduated from Portland State University with a dual major in business administration/finance and African studies) and car loans plus some reckless consumer spending threatened to overwhelm me. The awful sensation of being at someone else's mercy haunted me. The situation seemed more than a little ironic, too. I was living paycheck to paycheck while working as a financial consultant.

Up to this point I had lived my life a certain way and followed the rules as they were set before me: Get as fine an education as possible or learn a trade. Seek a good job and work hard at it. After earning a bachelor's degree I followed the path shown to me and ended up running into a lot of financial trouble. Sadly, I was very familiar with this route. When I was growing up my family didn't have any money so it wasn't surprising that I was clueless where creating, using, maintaining, or respecting money were concerned.

Still, I felt that no matter what happened I could get by even as I sought a way out of what promised to be a long haul.

Then, in the summer of 2001, a colleague recommended *Rich Dad's CASHFLOW Quadrant* to me. It didn't take me long to realize that I was on to something very important. I had enlisted in the United States Marine Corps after college and I knew about the process of following directions and getting results. As in the military, Rich Dad's material provided a simple, effective, and efficient strategy that anyone from any background could learn, implement, and get positive results from. I was amazed at how easy the steps and exercises were and, later on, the incredible results they yielded.

Rich Dad's Retire Young, Retire Rich was next on my reading list. I ordered the *Choose to Be Rich* course and by November I had done all the exercises and filled in all the financial statements. This process proved invaluable. I could clearly see where I was—and was not—financially.

What particularly intrigued me about the course was the information on how to leverage both the strengths as well as the weaknesses of all kinds of investments. The disastrous events of September 11 accelerated my sense of urgency and recognizing that I was on the right track. I picked up *Real Estate Riches* by Dolf de Roos and used the *Rich Dad's Road to Riches* (6 Steps Real Estate) course. I also attended a one-day seminar, featuring the Rich Dad's advisors, in Arizona. That's where I clearly understood that: a) I could choose to be like everyone else who carried heavy debt for years, or b) I could choose to turn my situation around to my advantage. And I could do it fast.

About two months after beginning the *Choose to Be Rich* course, I started to take control of my life. I restructured my current financial situation and without changing my budget I was able to save $400 more a month and start giving $200 to charity by following the "How to Get Out of Debt" formula.

I can say with total honesty that taking control was the most powerful and fulfilling feeling I ever experienced. At that point I knew I was the captain of my own ship that was sailing toward the future I always dreamed about, a world filled with things to do and see. Life offers so much, and using time wisely is the best way to take advantage of it. Putting my life on hold while I paid old bills wasn't an option any longer.

Change Happens

Facing personal obstacles isn't easy, but it's a mighty powerful feeling when you manage them instead of the other way around. First, I confronted a bad habit, which was buying into the negative attitudes of colleagues because I worried what they would think about me. With mostly good intentions, more than a few people expressed their views that what I planned to do, namely end my slow pace in the rat race, was foolish if not destructive. But my awareness that getting ahead financially and changing the quality of my life, even with a good job, was impossible without major interventions, superseded their reservations.

When I explained my newfound definitions of assets and liabilities, my credibility was compromised. That was tough to take at first, but I knew, deep inside, that the Rich Dad information was right.

With fresh perspective, my head cleared and I gained focus. Whereas pre–Rich Dad I thought risk involved investing money or taking an action without knowing what the outcome would be, now I recognized that risk could mean being informed and financially literate but still not taking action. Not taking any action to change my situation was a mistake. It was time to act.

First I opened a money market account and built up savings of $2,000. This short-term reserve would be shown to mortgage lenders if necessary. Then I followed the recommendation of Dolf de Roos and began to search for properties. I heard more than my share of, "You can't do that here." I countered with, "The properties are out there. They are waiting for me to find them."

Highly motivated, I looked at seventy-five properties in the Portland area and ran numbers on thirty of them. Out of these I found three or four good candidates and talked to property managers about them. One property, in addition to showing good numbers, also carried a tax abatement. I had found my first real estate investment property. I purchased the single-family residence in November 2002.

(Please don't get the idea that I am a one-man show. I put a team together to help me. It consists of a tax advisor, a real estate agent, a property inspector, and a personal attorney. I asked friends and acquaintances for referrals. I made use of the time I spent as an intern in a local bank and asked people who worked there about real estate agents and investment properties.)

With this first acquisition I moved from being a purely limited paper investor—I lost $5,000 in the stock market—to being a real estate investor.

I'm on a learning curve to building my wealth as I learn and boost my confidence even more. I'm twenty-five—and I don't want to wait any longer than I have to. I estimate two more years of self-employment and that within five years I will be able to live off my passive income and concentrate on investments. That plan includes attending business school in 2004 to earn my MBA.

Before taking control of my financial life I imagined I would retire at fifty or fifty-five. With no genuine game plan for the future, I figured, rather naively, that I would count on my schooling and intelligence to pull me along. I'm so relieved to say that I know better. Now I have a realistic plan in place that will allow me to retire at age thirty with a better standard of living that will constantly increase.

Additionally, I provide better financial planning for my clients using information I never heard of in business school. By recommending that they use the Rich Dad books and products, I give them the mechanism they need to get where they want to go. When they see that so much is available to them, they take advantage of them, too.

There's been another business change that reflects the difference in my financial perspective. I've shifted from one-time fees to services that earn me residuals. I understand that passive income keeps paying, whether I'm sitting at my desk in Portland or sitting on a beach in Tahiti.

Be Honest and Get On with Your Life

Being honest with myself was tough. Once I admitted that I hadn't made such great decisions in the past—overdoing personal spending was an excellent example—I allowed myself to move on. What happened in the past was over. Optimism kicked out the negatives and kicked into gear.

I've overcome self-imposed barriers about being too young, lacking the time, and having no experience in real estate investing. I've come to trust myself to read numbers and understand potential risks and returns. Reading through the material, doing the worksheets and exercises—these weren't hard to do. *When you're informed the way you need to be, taking action is easy.*

In the short time since I first read and implemented the Rich Dad course and materials, I went from/to the following:

Annual income:	$28,000 to $50,000
Passive income:	0 to $4,000–$6,000
Net cashflow per month:	$150 to $700
Bad debt:	$55,000 to $29,000
Monthly tithing:	0 to $300 or more
Liquid savings:	$100 to $3,500
Property:	none to owning one rental property

I use financial statements that I update at least weekly, which makes all the difference in the world. This simple management tool allows me to track my money as it comes in and goes out. All the guesswork about "Where did my money go?" is gone for good.

The biggest lesson I've learned is that now, as well as in the future, a person must be financially literate. I believe, as Robert does in *Rich Dad's Prophecy*, that a very dark and impoverished future is awaiting those who do not take charge of their financial lives right now. In the next decade a record number of baby boomers will be retiring and aging, spiking the need for medical care, which will likely remain expensive. That same population has already seen their 401(k) bubble burst, along with a decline in the value of their personal stock investments. Millions of people aren't saving enough for their retirement years and Social Security payments are not going to give them the financial cushion they will need.

But there *is* a choice. The average person—like me—can take control of his finances by deciding to do so. I've moved away from the edge of the financial pit and found solid ground. The magic to getting results and increasing the quality of life lies in the desire to change and the willingness to follow Rich Dad's simple strategies to becoming wealthy. This stuff works!

Chapter 17

Fast Learner

MICHELLE LABROSSE, PMP
East Hartford, Connecticut

"Rich Dad saved my life." I said this to Sharon Lechter when I met her at a Women Presidents Organization meeting this year and I meant it.

I had read the Rich Dad books and listened to the books on tape. The material basically gave me the guts to stop focusing on the bill collectors, which was a huge turning point because I put my focus on building my business rather than placating the bill collectors. When you spend a portion of every day consumed by how you're going to pay your bills, it's difficult to focus on how to best build a business.

Also, the Rich Dad books emphasized creating the processes and getting other people to do them. I had not delegated well prior to reading those books but after reading them, I realized the only way for me to grow was to learn how to let go. I also learned that I did really need to learn how to sell and made it a priority to develop mastery in sales. It's never any one thing that makes people successful, and the material presented in *Rich Dad Poor Dad* provided the elements that were missing in my ability to be successful.

Still, failure is a part of every success story. My adventures in business prove that this is true. Rich Dad helped me see what abilities I still needed to be successful. By focusing on my business, learning to delegate, and learning to sell, I was able to grow my business from $25,000 in year one to $250,000 in year two to $2.5 million in year three, all accomplished as a single mother.

The Early Years

With a full Air Force ROTC scholarship to cover my tuition at Syracuse University, I graduated with a BS in aerospace engineering and an MS in mechanical engineering. I began my professional career in 1984 as an Air Force lieutenant.

In 1987, at the age of twenty-five, I left the military to run my own consulting and training business because I knew that I wasn't suited for corporate life and my instincts paid off, at least in the short term. I earned very good money as an expert on how the environment impacted electronics. But my early success led to failure later on. I wasn't learning about cashflow management; instead I was distracted by the huge bump in income I was earning. In a very short time, I went from $20,000 a year to $150,000. Unfortunately, I wasn't developing the skills I needed for long-term success. I let the money lull me into a false sense of security.

Additionally, my husband and I disagreed about my entrepreneurial pursuits. I wanted to run my own company even if it meant short-term sacrifices. He thought I should give up my dream and be an employee. But after our first daughter was born in 1989, and the second in 1992, my focus shifted. Earning a lot of money wasn't as important to me as staying home with the girls.

By 1995 my marriage had broken up. I found myself raising our two young daughters by myself as well as covering the mortgage payments.

By 1997 I realized that I just didn't have things together to make it in my own business. Giving up on my dream, I sold the lakefront home outside Seattle that my former husband and I had built together and moved across the country from Washington state to Connecticut to be closer to my parents. Leveraging my degree, I took a job as a research scientist for a large aerospace company.

At the age of thirty-five I felt like a total failure. My dream of owning my own business had evaporated. To me, working for someone else did not mean being on my own. And I moved back east, which I hadn't wanted to do.

Then in March 2000, my position as a research scientist in systems engineering and adult learning was eliminated. Downsized, I saw this as an opportunity to start another company. I had negotiated the intellectual property rights of a course I had developed and taught over a year while a research scientist for the large aerospace company As was the case with many start-up companies, I was forced to bootstrap the initial funding. Credit card cash advances, along with the $40,000 I had saved in a 401(k) during my two and a half years as an employee, provided the money I needed. The first six months were a real struggle, a déjà vu of 1995 through 1997 when I was first on my own after being divorced. My daughters and I learned to live on a shoestring—there was no room for extras.

In November 2000 my brother suggested that I read *Rich Dad Poor Dad*. I did—and it saved my life. I immediately read the other Rich Dad books. Failure was about to take a back seat to success.

A Different Way Works

I applied the Rich Dad philosophy to how I ran my existing business by focusing on the creation of intellectual property such as patents.

To begin working on what Rich Dad refers to as the intellectual property asset column, I wanted to write a book based on the course that I had developed. I found a publisher and everything else fell into place.

My first book contract, on accelerated project management, was signed in December 2000. I knew that I needed certification as a project management professional (PMP) to give the book added credibility. The exam usually required six months of study but I didn't want to wait that long. I put together my own twenty-hour study program and marketed it. Then I used it, and passed the test with an excellent grade. Next, I started teaching the method in a course where people spend four days with us and on the fifth day they take the very difficult certification exam for project managers. Using these techniques, we became, in less than a year, the largest provider for this type of training out of a competitive pool of sixty-five providers and captured about 25 percent of the market in less than eighteen months

By March 2002 my book was published and the first licensee of my training products in India was launched. Both the book and foreign license provided me with passive cashflow. As Robert's rich dad would say, "My intellectual property assets were working for me."

Two months after signing my book contract, the credit card bills that I used to finance my business were completely paid off. I also put far more emphasis and focus on managing cashflow and got rid of my credit cards as a means of short-term capitalization of the business.

Robert Kiyosaki tells a story in one of his books about making more sales so that they could afford a copier; that really resonated with me. Instead of financing my business needs on credit, I switched to financing my business needs based on increased sales.

The company holds no credit cards and I will not set up lines of credit to cover hard times. Here's how we do business: In May 2002 a vendor who was doing our event registrations held $100,000 of our revenue as operating cash. In two weeks, through aggressive sales activity, we boosted our cash reserves. That period of time proved to me that the best way to handle cashflow crises is with sales, not lines of credit. As rich dad said, "The number one skill in business is the ability to sell."

The business has increased in revenue ten times every year for the past three years. Here's how enormous a change this is: In 2000, my first year of business, my associates and I earned a whopping $25,000. The second-year income rose to $250,000. Last year, the earnings surged to $2.5 million.

Twenty-five people are employed by my company in five locations around the country. We also license our training products overseas. Licensing to companies, and customizing the product to each one's particular need, is another important aspect of the business, as it leverages the original intellectual property by creating new revenue streams.

I Changed My Approach, and My Business Changed, Too

Pre–Rich Dad, I limited the growth of my business because I would not ask people to help me. Also, I didn't let go of things. Trained as a systems engineer, I taught numerous courses on creating business processes. I had the skill to produce the business systems that would bring me success but I couldn't let go. I had to learn to stop playing Superwoman. I realized that my job was to create the systems, make sure they functioned reliably, and get out of the way. Knowing that I had to be more disciplined about business processes, I hired professional talent to run the day-to-day operations so that I could focus on new products and business development.

The most important perspective change I picked up from the Rich Dad information was to focus on building up my assets and not being so worried about paying my bills. This doesn't mean that I didn't pay my bills. Of course I did. But in contrast to how I thought pre–Rich Dad, now I concentrate on what is most important to my business.

Where risk was concerned, my perceptions shifted as well. Since the mid-1980s, when I was a reliability engineer, I used a very engineering- and project-management-oriented definition. Risk was the probable chance that a negative event was going to happen that would prevent me from reaching a goal. Then I had to figure the impact on reaching the goal if in fact that negative event occurred.

Today, risk to me means jumping into a business area that I know nothing about and sinking a ton of money into it before I've learned how to create the system that will work. Rich Dad helped me see how to systemize my due diligence in opening a new business. This helps minimize the risks. I use a five-tiered approach to reduce risk:

1. *Concept.* This is the opportunity, the size of the market, strength of competitors, and cost to develop products.

2. *Development.* Here I take the "cookie cutter" approach, and look for an already existing model or formula that will fit.

3. *Product Launch.* This is the early marketing stage to ascertain what people do and don't like about the product.

4. *Market Launch.* This is the time when sales and marketing implement what has been learned.

5. *All Systems Go.* The know-how to sell and market the product is in place, but the process doesn't stop there. Constantly improving the product is part of it, too.

On a Personal Note

Perhaps most significantly, on a personal level, my relationship with my family has changed, too. Years ago, when my big dreams fueled my business aspirations my family thought I was, well, nuts. I was a single mom and my family felt responsible for me. Also, my mother's father had been an entrepreneur, and she remembered the boom-and-bust years very well. Now I'm regarded as a mentor.

While they still think I'm crazy, they are in awe of what I've managed to do over the past two years. Better yet, they are actively supportive, each in his or her unique way.

My goals include selling my businesses within the next five years, allowing me to retire. Nonetheless, I never really think in terms of retirement. I am doing what I love to do, enjoy the free use of my time, and go on vacation wherever I want, whenever I want. I love having more time to spend with my children. Yet I am continually excited about the pursuit of new goals.

My Lessons

I learned to develop the skills I needed so that what I love can bring me a ton of money.

I stay focused and created monetary goals for myself.

There is no such thing as job security. The only security I will ever attain must be developed from learning how to successfully run my own business.

Don't give up. If one venture fails, I'll know what it takes to do it better the next time.

Find out what I need to be successful and set up my own rules.

Be who I am.

Surround myself with people who support me and can give me good advice.

Remember that success drops clues. Follow the trail.

I can start being smart anytime I want to. (The flip side applies, too. I can stop being stupid anytime I choose.) I can turn failure into success.

Chapter 18

No Limits

TERRI BOWERSOCK
Tempe, Arizona

I met Robert Kiyosaki five years ago at a conference where we were both speakers. Listening to what he had to say, I related to Robert because we both had experienced problems in school. I had trouble reading and spelling. Second, I realized that I had to make changes in my business. When I returned to my office I told my CEO about what I had heard and suggested that he read *Rich Dad Poor Dad.* Then I said, "We need to own buildings."

Before I heard about Rich Dad I thought that all I had accomplished was the best I could do. Rich Dad showed me that life had an even bigger picture for me. To show you just how amazing that is, you should know that I'm the founder and owner of Terri's Consign & Design Furnishings, a nationwide company that sells all kinds of new and used furniture. I had already come a long way and achieved quite a lot of success. Rich Dad helped me to go places I couldn't have imagined.

The Early Years

Dyslexia, a learning disability, made me feel different and stupid. All through school, big red teacher comments like "Poor Work" or "Lazy" were scrawled across my papers. By the fifth grade, I started using slapstick humor to get through the day. My teacher would pick up a yardstick and pretend to play pool on the back of my head as he said, "You are as dumb as a cue ball." It hurt me deep inside, but I didn't let it show. Instead, I would play off the pain as I shouted, "Eight ball in the corner pocket!"

But all my joking didn't change the fact that by the time I left school I knew I was in for a hard time. I couldn't fill out a job application. Even with my poor reading skills, I could tell that my applications were riddled with misspellings. I was a twenty-one-year-old woman who turned in the work of a third-grader. I was so afraid to give something in writing because I knew that the reader would assume I was dumb. A lump developed in my throat at the thought of having an interview.

I even tried to be a waitress, but I couldn't spell "kofie."

Out of frustration, I decided to take time off from job hunting in Arizona and visit my father in Kansas. While sitting on the plane I considered my future. "What future?" I thought bitterly. I would never be able to have a career. With tears in my eyes, I prayed that no one would start talking to me for fear I would burst out crying.

The answer about my future came to me when my father took me to visit a friend of his named Betty. Betty operated the Clearing House Consignment Shop. I saw sterling silver, china, small furniture, and knickknacks displayed there. People were actually having fun as they purchased what others no longer wanted! Betty graciously explained how she managed the business. By the time she was done explaining, I knew I could do it, too.

My mind took off in a million directions. I started visualizing how my store would look. By midnight, I had my business all figured out. I jumped out of bed and called my mom to tell her about our new adventure. "Mom, we're going to be rich!" I told her. With great enthusiasm, I explained the whole idea.

She immediately responded, "You mean we are going to be like *Sanford & Son*? We are going to haul junk and sell used furniture? I'm going back to sleep."

The next day, I concentrated on a way to convince Mom that a consignment store was our ticket to success. I drew up a business plan to help her understand what I wanted to do. It wasn't a typical business plan. I created mine with crayons and colored pencils. Designing my success, I actually drew how the store would look. When I got home and explained to her what I wanted to do, she was convinced that the plan could work.

Mom and I borrowed $2,000 from my grandmother and set out to make my vision a reality. Climbing on my motorcycle, I went to find a store location. I saw a "For Lease" sign and went in to chat with the owner. After agreeing to the monthly rent, I was handed the lease to sign. Unable to read the legal jargon, I faked reading it by estimating how long it would take a normal person to read it. Then I signed my name. Presto! I was in business! I set up a bed in the back of the store.

I talked my mom into giving me her living room furniture along with my childhood bedroom furniture. My first sale at Terri's was the mirror from my set. When the buyer said, "I'll take it," I was so thrilled that she had to remind me to add in the sales tax.

From that first sale in 1979, Terri's Consign & Design Furnishings grew into a multimillion-dollar-a-year business. With sixteen stores, it is the largest consignment furniture chain in the country. These 20,000 square foot stores are filled with new and gently used fine furnishings from homes like yours, as well as from estates, model homes, and liquidations. And I kept my promise to Mom. It is not *Sanford & Son*.

Word of the company's growth spread like wildfire, aided by my inspirational speaking, which let people know that if I could do it, so could they. As a result of the increased exposure, I began winning national awards including one from *Inc.* magazine for the 1992 Retail Entrepreneur of the Year. In 1994 I won the Blue Chip Enterprise Award from the U.S. Chamber of Commerce. In 1998, I was given the Avon Woman of Enterprise Award. That award, along with a story about me in the *National Enquirer*, led to an appearance on *The Oprah Winfrey Show*. So perhaps you can see why I thought that I had reached the pinnacle of my success.

But when I heard what Rich Dad had to say I not only realized that many more opportunities beckoned, I realized that I could take advantage of them. Pre–Rich Dad I paid cash for everything, including rent, equipment, and trucks. With Rich Dad I learned how to leverage what I had so that it could be used to create cashflow.

Here's How I Did It

Rich Dad said that a person has to become an investor as well as a business owner to become rich. Before Rich Dad, I had leased most of my stores. After listening to Robert I realized that I should be investing in real estate so that I could make investments that would provide financial security.

So with my CEO Kevin Crippa's help, the company bought five acres of land. The location was great and we grabbed it knowing that others would want it. We used $225,000 of company money for the down payment and took out a loan from the bank for an additional $225,000. Rich Dad says to use the bank's money to create cashflow and that's what we did.

We then traded the land and formed an LLC (limited liability company) joint venture with a developer; they constructed a 73,000 square foot office building. The developer paid us back our original $225,000, assumed the loan on the land, and gave us 21 percent ownership of the building, which is now filled with tenants and cashflowing nicely.

Next we leveraged our $1 million worth of equity in this joint venture to secure 100 percent financing to construct a second building and leased it to our store. We have continued to leverage our equity position in each of our properties in order to build three more stores that we own. We have plans to build two additional stores over the next two years.

We are going to pull cash out of those last two buildings. First, we will purchase raw land. Next we will sell or trade that land into a joint venture. Then the joint venture will develop the land, which will increase its value. The joint venture will also establish leases for the property. Finally, the joint venture will obtain permanent long-term financing. At that time we will be able to pull cash out.

After five years we will own six buildings. In the past five years I made more money in real estate than I did in twenty-three years in the furnishings business. If I sold my furnishings business the real estate could support me.

I have also branched out to own other businesses. For instance, Terri's Consign & Design Furnishings is being licensed to the national level using the concept of "trading in" furniture. While developing this new idea, we realized that we needed the software that would support the consignment industry.

So we recently invested in FurnServe Software Inc., which has the only software program that supports the consignment segment. With this software we designed an exclusive consignment and trading system used by Terri's Consign & Design licensees. We did a trade: We get use of the software and the computer company gets equity in what we're going to do with it. Before meeting Robert Kiyosaki for the second time, I had bought a portion of the company.

When I saw Robert recently it was at the Pat McMahon morning talk show in Phoenix, where we were both guests. After Robert listened to my interview, he invited me to attend one of his seminars. After going to the seminar my reaction was *Wow!* I saw that owning the software company made sense because I could license the software. I bought more of the company.

The seminar also showed me why buying homes and renting them made such good sense because they created cashflow. So I also started another company with two other people. We purchase houses, furnish them with items from Terri's Consign & Design Furnishings, and rent them.

Currently I am concentrating on licensing my company's name, the concept of "trading in" furniture, and the consignment software. Our annual revenues, including the furnishings business, now exceed $55 million.

With Rich Dad's guidance I used other people's money and ideas and applied them to generate greater success in my own business.

I've Come a Long Way

Without dyslexia I would never have found my entrepreneurial spirit. Today, through motivational speaking and my books, I inspire others to reach beyond their limitations. I have made a commitment to give back to society and to be an inspiration to others by sharing my belief: You can succeed if you believe in yourself!

Without Rich Dad I wouldn't have known that everything is affordable. A person doesn't have to be rich to follow his principles, just willing to learn about what is possible. And then go and do it. (A good lesson we learned is that if a bank you've done business with for a long time starts to produce too much red tape tell them you'll shop around.)

With Rich Dad I learned how to work smarter and not try to run everything myself. I followed Rich Dad's teachings and surrounded myself with a strong advisory team.

I know that the buildings I own will fund my retirement. Not having to worry about my future finances lets me breathe easier. Even better, I can expand into other interests, including speaking, which has turned into yet another business.

Thank you, Rich Dad, for your inspiration!

Part VI

Life-Changing Events

One of the most profound lessons my rich dad taught me was to master the power of money and not be afraid of it. Many people become slaves to money because they are afraid of not having enough of it. To try to combat that fear they seek high-paying jobs. Instead of figuring out how money can work for them, they work for money.

He also told me about people who lived in poverty. Fear of and ignorance about money troubled them, too.

In this section you'll meet people from both sides of the fear coin: those who earned a lot of money and one who didn't work at all. All of them used Rich Dad information as a way to overcome their money fears to build strong financial futures.

First, you'll read how a woman overcame amazing odds. Stacey Baker, who lives in New Zealand, lived in poverty for part of her life, grew up only to go on welfare, and seemed to have few, if any, prospects for improving her financial life. Yet, she used the Rich Dad resources to take control and create cashflow. Her story is a great example of showing how it isn't necessary to have money to make money. Financial literacy, on the other hand, is necessary and helps you see opportunities right in front of you.

In contrast to Stacey's inspiring story, I've received e-mails from people who spent years building their careers because the power of money, to them, came from an ever-increasing paycheck. Job security was enormously important, as were promotions and perks. But they came to realize that their behavior was driven by the fear of not having enough money. They recognized that pay raises weren't the formula for financial security. The more money they earned, the more they spent. The more successful they became, the busier they were, resulting in less and less time for their family and friends. They couldn't rely on the money they made to sustain them when they eventually retired. For one thing, they were spending a lot of it because they assumed there would always be more. For another, they did not have assets that would create cashflow that could support them. Their physical body was their only asset.

When they learned through Rich Dad how to acquire assets that would provide them with long-term cashflow, they changed the way they thought and behaved. The fear of not having enough money evaporated. Worries about job security and debt were replaced by confidence about steady cashflow provided by assets.

In this section you'll meet Yong-Sik Shin, a dedicated corporate employee in Korea whose concern about money is combined with his frustration over the difficulty in advancing in his company. With Rich Dad as his guide, he sets his sights on different goals, starts his own business, and discovers that he can control his finances. His finances don't control him any longer.

Here, too, is California resident Ronald Hoard, right on the edge of retirement. Big salaries were a constant in his professional life but as he neared fifty he began to take stock of his financial future. The Rich Dad information gave him the financial education and the self-confidence he needed to plan for the years ahead. For anyone whose previous investments have disappointed him or her and who's concerned about being able to retire, follow how Ronald, helped by Rich Dad, took control of his financial security.

Finally, Michael Maritzen, who also lives in California, tells his amazing story. A highly paid corporate executive who had everything—including a lot of debt—he totally reconstructed his financial life. In his case, his biggest motivation was surviving one of America's most catastrophic events.

If you do not want to work hard for the rest of your life, no matter where you live, or what your financial circumstances are, you, too, can take charge of your financial education and change your life.

Chapter 19

Greener Pastures

STACEY BAKER
Auckland, New Zealand

Not very long ago, my self-description would go like this: thirty-year-old high school dropout, single mother, welfare recipient. Stuck in the bad habit of what I called "poor think," I feared change because I didn't know any better. Struggling to get out of an emotional and financial maze, I lived a demoralizing life.

But I was lucky because I discovered Rich Dad knowledge about what was possible financially, even in my dire straits. Paying attention changed my situation. My confidence grew so that I could consider, and act, on new and exciting options.

Today I own a thriving medical practice and two rental properties. I choose not to work. Instead, I prefer to construct a financially secure life for my son and myself while we enjoy ourselves along the way.

The Way It Was

Although Mangere, where I was born in 1966, was synonymous with gardens, in reality the area was just like any other suburb of Auckland. Middle-class citizens who worked full-time jobs lived there. Everyone owned a house on a quarter acre of land and minded their own business. Our house was surrounded by farmlands, which over the years were swallowed up by the urban sprawl of an ever-increasing population.

My father ran a small business. He created a company that built large greenhouses up and down the length of New Zealand's North Island.

As children, we were not expected to deal with money. The only times I had any occurred when the market prices for the tomatoes that we grew on our property were low. Then Dad would set up a roadside stall beside our front gate. Either one of my six siblings or I worked there. Occasionally my father would be a little lax about emptying the money box and we'd be able to collect enough spare change to buy a bottle of Coke or some sweets. Then, when I was seven, my parents separated. All the children moved out of the house with our mother.

Although my mother took the odd part-time job after the separation she still had young children to raise and qualified for welfare. My recollections of those times are of poverty and being cold (I can still see my myself as a child, trying to warm my hands under the hot water tap one winter). The house we lived in was in a dreadful state. I remember waking up in the morning, in the bedroom that I shared with my mother, a brother, and a younger sister, and putting my feet down on a freezing, wet floor. The frayed carpet was soaked from a very bad leak in the plumbing system.

Money problems also plagued my father, and I watched as he made one uneducated business mistake after another. He believed that hard work was its own reward and he was fanatical about teaching that to his children. He never bothered to look at his bookkeeping and was forever doing things for others for free. One of my most painful memories concerns him. It's hard being a kid and watching your father actually cry over money. But that happened twice when he edged perilously close to bankruptcy.

My siblings and I struggled along, completely naive about money. All we knew about money was that we saw very little of it.

Things were tough for me at school, too. Because of where I lived, I really thought that I would never amount to anything. From the day I began primary school I could not keep up and I knew that I was not going to be a successful student, the kind who studies and hands in homework when it was due. Playing held a lot more interest for me. That and lunch.

By the time I was in high school I was assigned to the "dumb" class. However, I did find one subject I liked and did well in. Physical education was fun. But I also enjoyed hiding under a tree to smoke cigarettes.

Not being present became the norm. When I noticed that my name was missing from the roll in geography, my last class of the day when I was fifteen years old, I just went home early. Ironically, when I took my end-of- the-year exams I received my highest mark in the subject. Of course, I still failed all my classes. I couldn't stand school. To me it was irrelevant, a joke.

My ambitions were as narrow as the lines on a highway. When a teacher asked me what I wanted to do after I left school, I told her I wanted to be a truck driver. But I did have a fallback position. If my first choice didn't work out then I could always get a job in a factory. I didn't even make it that far.

At sixteen I dropped out of school and became a mail sorter for New Zealand Post. I figured that was as good as it was going to get. The world was closed to me.

My Money Woes Begin

By the time I was twenty-three I was carrying credit card and loan debt of around $30,000 due to my complete ignorance about money. I was earning all of $250 a week doing some completely unmemorable job (there was quite a string of jobs like that). By the age of thirty I was a single mother on welfare living in a rented space with a friend. I spent my time trying to get more money out of the government instead of trying to create my own income.

It was a very scary time, the lack of money was terrifying. With no prospects and a little person to support, I felt overwhelmed. I remember worrying about paying my boy, Weston's, kindergarten fees, which were about $10 a week. That's how bad things were.

I was still on welfare in 1997 when I heard about *Rich Dad Poor Dad* through a current affairs TV program called *The Holmes Show*. Robert was being interviewed, and he also talked to schoolchildren. What struck me was his opinion that a house wasn't an asset. What he said made sense.

My flat mate, who was a medical doctor, watched the interview, too. A short time later we noticed the book in a shop and she purchased it. My friend was halfway through some other book so I read it first and found myself relating to the text. Wanting to know more, we decided to split the cost of CASHFLOW 101. We sent away for it and once the game arrived we began playing in earnest.

As I played, I began to understand that there were ways to better my situation—and I wanted to find them. Now, when people pointed out, yet again, that I was uneducated, poor, and a single mother on welfare, I realized I wasn't "stuck." Because of Rich Dad, I found that my thought process was changing, and much for the better.

And then my life took quite a turn. In 1998, my friend was offered the chance to buy the practice in which she worked. The business, which had been running for around ten years, had completely funded itself and still turned a profit. But she said that she wasn't interested as there was another practice she thought about going into. Suddenly I realized something.

I saw an opportunity, the likes of which I had never noticed before, right in front of me: *We could buy the medical practice.* With new knowledge guiding me, I told her so. Sitting down together, we talked and wondered about how we could do it. Neither of us had any money.

Here's How We Did It

The price the owner was seeking wasn't a secret. He had written it down—$400,000—when he approached my friend. Undaunted, my friend went back to him, informed him of our interest, and asked him how we could buy the business.

It turned out that the owner would be happy with $100,000 up front. If we came up with that amount of money, he told us, he would vendor-finance the rest. That meant that he would effectively act as a bank. After giving him the deposit, we would pay the remaining amount to him from the funds received from the business over the next two years.

My friend and I became partners. Since she had been offered the business in the first place and was a physician and I had recognized the opportunity through Rich Dad and pointed it out to her, we decided to go 50/50. We would share the risk of the $100,000 down payment and the $300,000 vendor-finance loan.

Next, we hired an accountant to put the numbers together, including the very important fact that the clinic turned over $1 million a year. Then, because my newfound business partner was a medical doctor, we went to the New Zealand Medical Assurance Society. This is a company set up to lend money and provide insurance for health professionals.

Explaining what we wanted to do, we presented the financials to the loan officer. This was a new experience for me, and I was more than a little nervous. After all, I had no money, I was still on welfare—and here I was, asking for a $100,000 loan! I need not have worried. When we presented the financials our loan was approved right away. The term of the loan was three years, with an interest rate of about 9 percent.

Everything kept moving very quickly. The sale was handled through lawyers (the seller's and ours) and the business paid for the closing costs.

The day we purchased the clinic I went off welfare. With great joy I turned to the next phase of my life.

We paid the $100,000 back over three years and paid the vendor-finance loan of $300,000 back over two years. At the same time the clinic always earned a tidy profit.

In 2002 my partner offered me her share of the business because she wanted to try a totally different lifestyle. My partner wanted $252,000. The business manager took on 25 percent of the business share as an incentive. We bought my partner's share with vendor financing, so we didn't have to come up with the money ourselves. Instead, we used profits from the medical practice. I now own 75 percent of the business. I do not spend time on the premises, as I am not medically trained. Instead, I attend to my next venture, investing in real estate, which, as Rich Dad says, is a great way to get cashflow.

Here's How I Did It

I began a business in which to buy real estate in August 2002. I paid my accountant $450 to set up the legal requirements.

Then I started to look for properties. I found a real estate agent who I really hit if off with and explained what I wanted. I told her I would be running numbers on lots of properties through my property investment software program, which defines ratios of cost verses equity and cashflow, until I found what I was after. If I didn't see enough equity and a positive cashflow then I would not make the investment.

So warned, the agent propelled properties my way. Sometimes, if one did not meet my criteria I would put in a lower offer. (In fact, every offer I've made has been much lower than the asking price.) Some would come back with a surprisingly low counteroffer. Then I'd know I was in. The others I let drop.

When the numbers worked—price, cashflow, and equity—the way I wanted them, I would then fax them to my property consultant, who is a mortgage broker. We'd talk about the property and if he liked it, too, then he arranged a mortgage for me.

To set up mortgages, I used some of the equity in my share of the medical practice. *I never put any of my own money into my properties.* Both of the following mortgages are fixed for three years, at a rate of about 7 percent. After that period of time is up I will get advice on how to continue from my consultant/mortgage broker. (In New Zealand, most mortgages are fixed for only two to three years.)

So far, two rental properties are mine. Both properties are positively geared, which means that each one shows a profit after all expenses and mortgages are paid.

The first house I purchased was a very large four-bedroom.

Purchase price: $221,000

Cash put into property

Down payment:	$25,000
Closing costs paid by me:	$0
Repairs/renovations paid by me:	$0
	$25,000

Monthly cashflow analysis

Rental income:	$1,950
— Vacancy loss (I don't deduct a vacancy loss because there is a housing shortage here at the moment.):	$0

Monthly expenses:

— Taxes (property):	$99.72
— Insurance:	$41.67
— Repairs and maintenance:	$50
— Reserve:	$0
— Management fee:	$0
— Loan payment (3 years at 7%):	$1,141.12
	$1,332.51
Net monthly cashflow:	$ 617.49

Annual cash-on-cash return

Annual cashflow ($617.49 × 12)	$7,406.88
÷	
Amount of cash put into property	$25,000
Cash-on-cash return	29.6%

On top of that, the software I use calculates depreciation into the equation. At the end of year I claim a depreciation loss and receive a tax rebate, which actually raises my monthly cashflow.

In 2003 the property was appraised at $235,000.

The second house contains two bedrooms and cost me $105,000.

Purchase price: $105,000

Cash put into property

Down payment:	$10,000
Closing costs paid by me:	$0
Repairs/renovations paid by me:	$0
	$10,000

Monthly cashflow analysis

Rental income:	$1,040
— Vacancy loss: (I don't deduct a vacancy loss because there is a housing shortage here at the moment.)	$0
Monthly expenses:	
— Taxes (property):	$88.06
— Insurance:	$33.33
— Repairs and maintenance:	$50
— Reserve:	$0
— Management fee:	$0
— Loan payment (3 years at 7%):	$524.37
	$695.76
Net monthly cashflow:	$344.24

Cash-on-cash return

Annual cashflow ($344.24 × 12)	$4,130.88
÷	
Amount of cash put into property	$10,000
Cash-on-cash return	41.3%

In 2003 the property was appraised at $130,000.

Since I've only been at it since August 2002 I think I'm doing quite well.

Sometimes, You Have to Fail

But I must admit that not every investment has been as rosy. In 2000, using dividends from the medical practice, I started an organic food and product business from scratch because the idea interested me.

After two years with no profit I walked away with a loss of several hundred thousand dollars. How did this happen? I kept loading money onto a sinking ship. In retrospect, I could have taken the $370,000 I invested, set it on fire, and witnessed the same result. My lesson was never to go into any sort of venture without having lots of knowledge about it. Because this business was started from scratch there was no structure or financial history, much less books or figures to look at.

When buying a business that is already operating one has the luxury of being able to look at the figures and calculate whether or not it is a good investment. What I did was basically a silly gamble—and I don't even like gambling.

I chalked this up as a very expensive and rather painful lesson. But I also kept thinking that there aren't many people who can walk away from this kind of deep financial loss and still be able to carry on and do well. And that's what I do, and I don't do it alone.

My Team Is on My Side

As Rich Dad suggests, my team is composed of experts in their areas who provide the detailed information I need. In this instance my limited education works in my favor. I figure I don't know anything about real estate investments so I hire people who do. I ask a lot of questions and they take the time to explain things to me. Therefore, my risks are minimized.

My team, which evolved, consists of:

- Property consultant (also a mortgage broker), who double-checks each deal for me.
- Real estate agent, who knows what I'm looking for and helps me find properties that fit my criteria.
- Building inspector, who checks the properties for building standards and informs me if any repairs are needed.
- Building valuer, who tells me exactly what each property is worth.

By the way, I still can't manage basic addition and subtraction, let alone the times tables. But I own quite a good calculator. So I guess you could say that I take calculated risks!

More seriously, understanding the difference between good debt and bad debt has contributed to the enormous difference in my life. I've learned from Rich Dad that good debt means buying assets that I never have to pay for and bad debt means buying doodads that lose value the minute I pay for them. Understanding this concept has brought me to a wonderful place. I have never been so well off.

Making the right choice and building from there is the formula I used to get me from where I was to where I am. And I'll tell you, I'd much rather be where I am now.

Where I'm Going Next

I don't have to work, which is a big change from not being able to get a decent job. My money works for me. Still, I intend to keep buying real estate, increasing my passive income, and building up equity. In a year from now I would like to own another five rental properties. Five years from now I plan to be investing in commercial property, including apartment houses.

I've learned not to listen when people tell me, "You can't do that here." I've had real estate agents refuse to put my offers to sellers because they thought my prices were too low. (I also had people tell me, when I voiced my desire to buy the medical practice, that I could not purchase it the way I intended to do it. They were mistaken, too.)

Perhaps the most miraculous, far-reaching effect of what has happened to me is the most internal one. Now I don't worry about money anymore. I feel secure because I know that if, for some reason, I lost everything I could make it again. Not relying on the government or anyone else gives me a very solid grounding. I feel that my son's future is much safer, at least where money is concerned. And that's wonderful.

He and I play CASHFLOW for Kids together. At the age of nine Weston knows about doodads (I keep reminding him), my rental properties, and the fact that I own a medical practice. He's already made money from some modeling jobs and he has a savings account. We'll see if he decides to invest it.

My single regret is that my parents didn't live to see what I'm capable of.

But my siblings, who still shake their heads in disbelief, are very proud of me. Some of my friends, with whom I shared the same leaky financial boat, have been motivated to seek the information they need to reach dry land and start over again. I'm so glad for them.

Today my son and I live northwest of Auckland, about ten miles from Mangere. Sometimes I drive through there. It is now a low socioeconomic area and I worry about the people living there. I wonder how they are going to provide financial security for themselves.

I know that I've come a long way against great odds. It gives me hope to know that they can use the same Rich Dad information I had, and join me.

Chapter 20

A Winning Strategy

YONG-SIK SHIN
Seoul, Korea

For years I had no source of income other than my salary and incentives. I received a bonus annually, at the year's end. It was calculated on the annual returns of the company, regardless of the employee's individual performance. The bonus normally amounted to 100 percent or 200 percent of my monthly pay.

Money provided a means to support my family in the present. But the future was a lot murkier. I wanted to make investments but I thought I could not afford them. Putting aside part of my salary for savings and a pension were the best I could do to protect my family from unforeseeable danger. So I deposited 30 percent of my salary and used part of it to repay a housing loan. I got the loan to lease a house for my family. Like so many others, we wanted to live in a better neighborhood, which would mean better education for our girls and finer living conditions for all of us. I am thirty-seven years old and my wife and I have two young daughters. But money problems existed, too. During one jobless period that lasted six months, I had to rely on a personal line of credit from the bank.

Where my views on my job and workplace were concerned, I believed that if I worked hard enough I would eventually become an executive before retiring at age sixty. I worked in the computer-game-related software industry since 1994. I had also been employed by both a large company and a venture business, working mostly in either the strategic planning or sales management departments. The strategic planning department concerned activities such as project development, examination (business analysis or managing business unit performance), and public relations (public-investor relations)

Like many in my generation, I felt that there was no other way to get through life other than by being an employee. Unfortunately, as a salaried person I was forced to face limitations, which included the seniority system in Korea. Until very recently in Korean society, such things as seniority, educational background, and connections, rather than one's ability, determined whether a person was promoted. It was no exception in the large company that I worked for and I was totally disillusioned by this fact. Even though I had made more distinguished contributions to the company than other colleagues or senior members, the rewards were not commensurate.

There was another problem that I had to face. Despite the fact that I had attended college, my degree was not from a so-called good school. Graduates of privileged universities actively exchange information and help out one another. Since I was not one of them, I missed out on that necessary information and I felt excluded.

But three years ago Rich Dad helped me to change how I worked, conducted business, and earned money. Most importantly, I altered how I lived my life—and how I looked at my future and that of my family.

The Guide I Needed, When I Needed It

Early in 2000, I came across a copy of *Rich Dad Poor Dad* in a bookstore. I was searching for a book on management but the cover caught my eye. I remembered that one of my senior friends had recommended the Rich Dad books, saying I should read them if I really wanted to be rich.

When I read the book, I related to the story about how difficult it was for salaried men to become wealthy. Working as a salaried man meant dealing with policies and rules that resulted in weakened creativity and a challenged spirit. And the fact that no rewards were guaranteed for performance, no matter how noteworthy, was dissatisfying.

I learned from reading *Rich Dad Poor Dad* that anyone could become rich with little money. At the same time I learned that I should have specific goals in my life. A truly rich man, I discovered, not only had a lot of money; he was warm and generous as well. Best of all, I realized that I could find the confidence to achieve what I wanted to do.

The Rich Dad message urging changes struck home because the situation I was in demanded changes. It took me less than an hour reading the book to come to that realization and take action. The first thing I decided to do was get to work at 7:30 A.M. when nobody else in the management level was in. The free time would give me several advantages. I could brace myself for another busy day, catch up on the news, and research information on the real estate market.

At home, I started to pay back the loans. Thanks to Rich Dad, the idea that the burden of debt might hinder my future plans forced me to repay the loans as soon as possible. I now have a personal line of credit and a minus account open in case of emergencies. A minus account is a loan account. I can withdraw money from it and deposit money into it. Although I have the account I have no intention of using it because I want to do without any loans as long as I can.

Finally, I made up my mind to retire before my fiftieth birthday as well as to become involved in my father's real estate business.

I had known that real estate was profitable because my grandfather was a self-made man who had made his own fortune using money that he had saved little by little to invest in properties. But after I read the Rich Dad books, I was able to come up with more specific and elaborate plans. I meticulously calculated the profitability of real estate projects and frequently consulted the model cases described by Rich Dad.

The Next Phase

At this time my father was suffering financial difficulty from debts. And although he was healthy, he was finding it more and more difficult to work. I suggested that he build a studio apartment building on a golf practice range that he owned.

Considering that my father could not afford an additional loan, the money for construction was supplied through the potential tenants. After obtaining bank loans, each one made a down payment upon signing of a contract for an apartment.

Joining up with a builder whose brand value was high was critical. Fortunately, the initial investment was rather small. The design of the apartment building cost only about $140,000 and we paid the lawyer's fee for a building permit. The plan was successful and I took care of selling the apartment units.

While doing that, I realized that I was more interested in and better at the real estate business than what I was doing to earn a salary. Starting my own business, which involved the development and management of real estate, I managed the studio apartment project for my father and developed other business ventures.

I was motivated by another Rich Dad message: If you have made up your mind about what you want to do, carry it out right away. Once I had my own business, I experienced a feeling of control over my time and work. Being creative and aggressive came naturally. This environment helped me come up with good ideas to gather better resources, both human and financial. Another plus was that my pay and benefits were better than before. Transportation, telecommunications, and other expenses were charged to the company.

Building the apartment house was more profitable than selling the land it stands on. So far 98 percent of the units have been sold. Each studio apartment measures between 450 and 570 square feet. Seven apartments and nine leisure rooms are reserved for later use.

The gross earnings from selling 388 studio apartments will amount to $32.6 million, while gross earnings from selling nine rooms for leisure facilities will amount to $2.75 million, totaling $35.35 million. After all expenses, including construction costs, taxes, advertising, and consulting fees, are paid, we will have a net profit of $5.15 million ($3.2 million goes to the landowner).

Now that I could see what my financial future could be like, I spent a year building my business before I left my "regular" job.

Other Investments Pay Off, Too

The Rich Dad books also affected the way I invested in the stock market. I began to realize the importance of assets and of raising seed money. I did the latter by putting aside part of my income. Also I began to use Internet-based financial asset management programs. They helped me make prudent investments.

I learned to seek long-term investments based on the accurate analysis of businesses and enterprises rather than the prospect of individual stocks. As I managed my investment patterns, I took into consideration economic policies, business environments, interest rates, exchange rates, and other factors. I have $41,000 reserved to invest in the stock market, but right now I am withholding it since the market condition is volatile.

I was fortunate because I learned from my own dad how to keep books on earnings and revenues. Ever since I was in elementary school I knew how to manage my money.

The Future Is Bright

I've learned—and continue to learn—about taking charge of my financial life. The Rich Dad information has taught me to always plan ahead and analyze what I'm doing, to make good use of the information from and the experience and opinion of my advisors (tax accountants and lawyers for instance). I am also following carefully the trends pertaining to financial and real estate markets and changes in related business environments in order to prepare for new real estate development projects.

If I sold all my assets now I would be able to come up with $840,000. If I placed this money in the bank, with the most conservative interest rate at 4.5 percent, I would receive about $3,100 a month minus taxes equaling 16.5 percent. However, since I have a family to look after I need more than that. So I will continue to acquire assets for my kids' education and my family's future.

My business is doing well and I enjoy gathering information and making decisions that will increase the profits from my investments. But what I enjoy even more is free time. I can decide when I want to work. That's a luxury that I never had as an employee. Perhaps not all that surprisingly, I've finally been able to overcome my personal obstacle of laziness. I used to procrastinate until a deadline came up, which sometimes got me into trouble. But now, with the incentive to build on what I've already accomplished supporting me, I don't want to miss out on any opportunity.

Chapter 21

On the Edge
of Retirement

RONALD HOARD
San Francisco Bay Area, California

As a Ph.D. who has worked for twenty-five years as a mechanical engineer in research and development for a government national laboratory, my system for keeping up with inflation was simple: work harder and then toil even harder still. I figured doing so would bring me promotions and impressive income. However, I didn't take into account that high-level jobs are far more stressful and unstable than entry-level and medium-income positions.

I also thought that maintaining a good management-level job was the only route to financial security. Prior to age thirty I figured that my government pension was sufficient, hence I held no other investments besides the now cursed 403(b) mutual funds. My wife and I lost approximately 60 percent—about $150,000—of our mutual fund accounts since the stock market collapse in 2000. I was a practicing yuppie, living from one paycheck to another.

But my mind was changed, and my world changed because of it. I no longer regard killing myself at work as a viable way to live, and especially not a reliable way to earn a lot of money. And while I'm employed as an engineer, my investments now include real estate in the form of multifamily apartment complexes. For my wife, our teenage son, and me, the path to financial security is already under our feet. We're on the road to a better lifestyle. Considering that I grew up in a Chicago ghetto, I'd say we're definitely headed in the right direction. Interestingly enough, playing a Rich Dad game was partly responsible.

A Board Game That Never Bores

One Saturday morning in 1999, my son, who is also named Ronald and was thirteen and a half years old at the time, and I sat down to play CASHFLOW 101. The year before we both read *Rich Dad Poor Dad* (the subtitle "What the Rich Teach Their Kids About Money—That the Poor and Middle Class Do Not!" was particularly attractive to me) and enjoyed it. When I saw the ad for the game in the back of the book I ordered it.

When we sat down to play, both of us were committed to sitting there until we escaped the rat race. It took a lot longer than we expected—and it was fraught with a bundle of unexpected emotions. Downsizing drove my son to tears. (It had the same effect on me. I just hid it from him.) It took everything I had to keep him—and myself—from becoming discouraged and quitting. Finally, eleven agonizing hours later, we finished the game. Despite the fatigue and emotional drain, I knew that something wonderful had happened to us.

Participating in the game broke through my biggest obstacle. I was always afraid to borrow money from the bank and plunge into debt in order to invest wisely in real estate. I was well aware of the adage, "It takes money to make money, but it doesn't have to be your own"—but I was afraid to do it. The necessity of reconditioning myself, to face the fact that borrowing money to buy properties was okay, was an enormously freeing event. I like to refer to the game as a "financial simulator/trainer."

I'm happy to report that the more we played, the better we became. We've been able to get out of the rat race in both CASHFLOW 101 and 202 in about an hour.

I Was on the Right Track All Along

Here's how much my perspective shifted. I already owned real estate. In 1983 and 1984 I bought two single-family condos in Stockton, California. These were priced at between $30,000 and $50,000, and we used cash as down payments. Shortage of cash restricted me to buying smaller deals back then.

Deciding to buy a larger house to live in, we rented out our old house. But neither the condos nor the rental produced positive cashflow (they did, however, provide tax advantages after their depreciation deductions).

But after I started reading the Rich Dad books, I realized that I could step up from the small deals to the next real estate level. Apartment units—big deals—were much more profitable. My thinking process expanded, as I understood that I could use the equities in the rental house and the condos to a much greater lucrative advantage.

By selling the properties we owned (not including the home we lived in) we would possess about $80,000 for down payments.

I started looking in California but concluded that none of the numbers made sense (big negative cashflows). Then I searched in Nevada (better) and Arizona (better still). Finally I located, on the Internet, a large apartment management firm based in Dallas, Texas. They managed about 30,000 units within the south-central United States (Texas to Oklahoma and Iowa to Virginia) and they also purchased and invested in apartment complexes.

With the direct phone number to their acquisitions manager in hand, I asked him where the markets were both reasonably priced and growing. He mentioned College Station/Bryan, Texas; Jackson, Mississippi; and Galveston, Texas, and gave me the number of a real estate agent in College Station. All three of my complexes are in that area.

We first purchased a thirty-seven-plex in Bryan for $425,000. While the building didn't look as attractive as some of the other local rentals did—it stood one story instead of two, and no balconies graced the outside—its low rents ensured steady occupancy. All the units were one bedroom and measured 400 square feet.

Here's the breakdown:

Purchase price: $425,000

Cash put into property

Down payment:	$85,000
Closing costs paid by us:	$6,000
Repairs/renovations paid by us:	$0
	$91,000

Monthly cashflow analysis

Rental income ($325/unit $\times$ 37):	$12,025
— Vacancy loss (5%):	$601.25
	$11,423.75

Monthly expenses:	
— Taxes (property) and insurance, utilities, yard, trash maintenance, and repairs:	$4,335
— Management fee (5% of rents):	$571
— Loan payment (25 years at 8.375%):	$2,709
	$7,615
Net monthly cashflow:	$3,808.75

Cash-on-cash return

Annual cashflow ($3,808.75 $\times$ 12)	$45,705
$\div$	
Amount of cash put into property	$91,000
Cash-on-cash return	50.2%

In 2003 the property was appraised at $669,000.

Since overcoming my fear of borrowing money, I used home equity loans on all of the apartment purchases. Two out of three apartment purchases I've made so far were entirely 100 percent financed.

The following year we purchased two more complexes in the same area, bringing our total number of units to 113. Their value is about $3.5 million. One immediately produced monthly cashflow; the other is going to be refinanced, which will produce cashflow as well.

To keep watch on my investments, I visit the properties every three or four months. Each time I meet with the property managers to talk over what needs to be done, walk through all vacancies, review work that has been done, and any other concerns involving the buildings.

The Next Phase

With experience and confidence gained from these investments, I'm going to do something exciting: My game plan is to use my government pension, which I'm eligible to draw as a lump sum on my fiftieth birthday, as a down payment on a much larger apartment complex. (The other option is taking the pension as an annuity, which would only give me a small monthly stipend.)

Leveraging this hefty lump amount will enable me to retire much earlier than most of my peers, who will stay, or try to remain, at their jobs until age sixty-five. Most of them will choose to do so because they need the income. Others, whose 401(k)s and other retirement investments disappeared in the last few years, will try to make up for lost time and income. A lot of them probably won't be able to keep their jobs until they reach sixty-five, as declining health, downsizing, and early retirement packages may force them out of work much earlier.

I've seen statistics about retirees that are very troubling. One aerospace industry study showed that the average person (aerospace employee) who retires at sixty-five lives an average of only eighteen months more. So the promised "lifelong" pension never gets paid. More importantly, a life snuffs out before retirement, and all the advantages it is supposed to bring—time, leisure, travel, less stress, visiting grandchildren—goes with it. It certainly seems like traditional retirement ages and the hard-won pensions that accompany them are not geared to the individual who worked thirty or forty years for them. This is not the scenario I want for my family and me.

The same studies also show that those people who leave their jobs sooner, say between the ages of fifty and fifty-five, enjoy a life expectancy that extends to an impressive eighty to eighty-five years. That's the choice for me. There's a whole lot of living to be packed into the next thirty-five years—at least!

But at the same time I want to say that my wife and I didn't decide to plunge my entire pension into real estate investing on a whim. We had a plan. Feeling that it was essential to gain experience first, we used our home equity funds to buy properties and started to invest three years before my retirement target date to gain the necessary experience. We kept our jobs while doing this, and learned to analyze investments as well as cope with the fears and anxieties that still cropped up.

I'll be honest: It is scary to move out of one's comfort zone. But stepping back and coolly going over the analysis of each property helps. So does knowing which past decisions have worked well, and which didn't. The cash-flow from our big deals gives us a soft cushion to fall back on, and that gives us confidence to keep investing in bigger deals. Our plan is to keep purchasing additional units every other year via refinancing.

And while I'm still surprised at how relatively easy it is to borrow money to purchase million-dollar investment properties, I remind myself that following the lender's rules is all it takes. Nonetheless, I never dreamed that I would be able to control such lofty sums of money. Growing up in a poor family, I never heard anything about how to obtain money (other than working hard for it), much less if we would ever amass large sums of it. Education was the key to creating all opportunities. But, while degrees helped me in my career, and the work I did provided me with the means to build on the investments I've already made, without a financial education I wouldn't have seen the real estate opportunities available to me.

To start, we intend to use $650,000 of my lump sum payout as a down payment for the next major real estate investment, either an apartment building or a small shopping mall. To do that, I'm working with a CCIM—certified commercial investment manager—in the Houston area who is combing the market in Texas and other areas, since he is also authorized to seek properties in other states. After all, my pension is riding on it!

Today I have the freedom and knowledge to consider options other than what I thought I had. I'm learning a lot along with my financial education, namely that a person must learn before he earns, but he eventually becomes what he studies (so pick interests, leisure activities, and hobbies carefully). Also, fear impedes learning, but knowledge conquers fear.

My team (property managers, real estate lawyers, real estate agents, a tax accountant, and lenders and bankers) helps me every step of the way. Their expertise goes a long way to dispelling fear. Also I strongly recommend using the services of large property management firms and CCIMs to help locate deals. Both are valuable members on any real estate investor's team.

An Investor in the Making

As my wife and I plan our retirement years, our son has carved out a new track for himself as well. While he previously intended to follow me into engineering, he has changed his mind. For one thing, he feels that engineers don't earn enough money. For another, by observing what we are doing—and still playing the CASHFLOW games—he has decided to major in real estate investment in college. He wants to become a CCIM, which will allow him to buy and sell the biggest properties, like skyscrapers and shopping malls. Unlike a lot of teenagers, at sixteen he is sure about what he wants to do and why he wants to do it. We're delighted with this development.

For those closer to my age, I want to say this: Start investing now and allow yourself at least three years to learn, make mistakes, and succeed. Don't wait until you're sixty-five, when the financial course of your life will be determined for you. Take charge of it now. If I had known at twenty what I know now, I would have been able to retire at thirty. I suspect that my son will.

Chapter 22

Second Chance

MICHAEL MARITZEN
Fremont, California

I was at Ground Zero on September 11, 2001. Like so many other Americans, I felt that I was an eyewitness to our world falling apart. I know that everyone deals with catastrophic events in their own way and in their own time. But I never imagined that a book—*Rich Dad Poor Dad*—could help me through such an unexpected ordeal. What enabled me, actually helped and focused me so that I was able to walk out of that wrenching trauma after I returned home, was Robert's message. I grabbed on to it and it pulled me from the emotional wreckage of what happened. This may sound unbelievable, but it's true.

Flying High Without a Financial Net

Maybe I was meant to read the book two or three months before September 11. As the chief architect of the Sony Corporation of America, my bicoastal job included business development, strategic planning, and creating and extending the Sony brand. To do this, I practically lived on airplanes. It wasn't unusual for me to board a plane to Japan, fly across the Pacific Ocean for a one-hour meeting, and turn around and fly home. On this particular day I was in Newark Airport after a business meeting, reading the *Wall Street Journal* while I waited for my flight. An article I was skimming mentioned *Rich Dad Poor Dad*, which caught my interest. Seeing the book at one of the airport bookstores, I bought one to read on the flight back to California.

This makes sense, I thought to myself as I read my way across the country. Robert wrote that the average person could change his or her life and become wealthy and attain freedom in the process. Being a financial wizard or a real estate broker wasn't necessary. The information was simple to understand, full of common sense, and yet powerful, too. Here was an action plan and the steps to make it happen. I recognized that there was a lot to learn but the payoff was huge—if I trusted myself.

What struck me was how Robert addressed fear. He understood that fear could act like a tidal wave, immobilizing you in its wake. To make sure that fear wouldn't overtake you any longer, he wrote about building confidence. Listening to other people telling you what you should or should not do was self-defeating. Trusting one's own instincts was the only way to go.

This lesson was soon taught to me in a way I'll never forget.

The Message Is Clear but I'm Not Listening

In retrospect, the universe seemed to be conspiring to convince me not to go to New York the days before September 11, but I wasn't really paying enough attention. The Saturday before, deep in the pit of my stomach, I felt that something terrible was going to happen. I knew without a doubt that there was a real chance that I would not come back from the scheduled trip. The weird thing was that my girlfriend was picking up the same vibe. And while we both worried, from time to time, about all my flying, this was different. We were filled with a dread the likes of which we had never experienced before.

Then I found out that the meeting was canceled. If that wasn't enough of a deterrent, the weather should have been. My flight was canceled. But I was determined to remain the dedicated corporate executive—there was always business to take care of in New York—so I booked another flight. That one didn't leave either. The third one did.

I was in the South Tower, on the seventeenth floor, when the first plane slammed into the North Tower. Everyone in my group decided to leave, and we started to walk down the stairs. Part of the way down, we saw people making their way back up. Despite their reassurances that everything was okay in our building, we continued downstairs. It was the instinctive thing to do.

When we made it outside I found myself standing next to a Japanese businessman. With all the chaos going on around me I heard only one relentless sound that was getting louder and louder. I looked up as the second plane hit the South Tower. Then I looked at the Japanese businessman and my adrenaline kicked in. Everything—my nerves, my instincts, my gut—was telling me to move, and move fast. But my companion was frozen to the spot. Now I'm not a tall man, but he was shorter than I was. I grabbed him under my arm and we started to run. We ran, eventually coated in the gray dust of destruction, until we reached the Sony building at 55th Street and Madison Avenue several miles away. We did not look back.

Leveraging Confidence = Leveraging Life

When I was finally able to get a flight back to California the following Saturday I was a mess. Yet I realized I was ready to make some major changes. First, I didn't want to spend the rest of my life on planes. Second, I believed I had reached the pinnacle of my career. I achieved everything in corporate life that I had set out to do. My job included impressive perks, a chauffeured limousine at my disposal, an open expense account, a six-figure salary, the latest techno toys—they were all mine. But now these things weren't important to me.

When I asked myself the big question: "What do I do now?" something bubbled up in my brain in reply. I remembered writing down, for the first time in my life, my objectives while I read *Rich Dad Poor Dad* what seemed like a lifetime ago. But I didn't do anything about them. At that time the ingrained way of thinking that I was brought up with took hold. "What if?" and "Yeah, but?" were mental rebuttals to my enthusiasm for Robert's information. The fact that one of my grandfathers went bankrupt investing in real estate many years before nagged at me.

But now everything was different. I was different. I intended to take control and live my life the way I wanted to. I sat down again and wrote out what I desired. I listed where I wanted to be financially and what I sought personally.

September 11 showed me that someday is right now.

The Structure I Knew

In my past, such keen self-awareness, much less action, was rare. Like a lot of people my age—I'm in my late forties—I was heavily influenced by the fact that one of my parents, in this case my mother, lived through the Depression. Growing up—I was born in Maine and grew up in Texas, where my Air Force father was stationed—my life was infused with fear. Losing a job, not being able to pay bills, or worst of all, going broke: There was so much to be afraid of. Getting a good education, working diligently at a job, and saving a small nest egg for retirement; that's what I was supposed to do, and that's what I set out to do.

I earned a master's in computer science at Texas A&M, and concentrated hard on building an impressive career. Still, I saw myself as an average Joe, trudging toward a retirement carrot in the very far-off future. Maybe when I was sixty-five I could stop working. Maybe not until I was seventy. Some days I thought maybe not ever.

I saved, too, just like I was taught to do. But the safety valve savings were supposed to provide failed me miserably. Between 1999 and 2002 I lost 75 percent of the value of my stock portfolio. My mutual fund portfolio declined 45 percent in worth. Between the two I lost more than $700,000. To top it off, my 401(k) plunged 30 percent in value, a dive that cost me close to $30,000. Suffering reversals nearing three quarters of a million dollars was a very troubling development, to say the least.

Things went from bad to worse. In 2001 my debt ballooned to more than $30,000 due to credit card spending and car payments. I actually borrowed from one credit card to pay off another. With all the money I earned, I still teetered on the edge of bankruptcy.

Rebuilding My Life

Soon after September 11, Sony began to eliminate projects and roles. I decided to take advantage of the situation and leave my job. Some of my friends, as well as my family, thought I was crazy. But I felt that I was doing what was right for me. A generous severance package allowed me to walk away from my old life while I mapped out a new one. In a very profound way I tapped into my recently discovered reserve of perspective. My plans revolved around me, not my job. I picked myself up physically, dusted myself off emotionally, and started over again mentally.

In October 2001, I accepted a job at a small software company where I did, and continue to do, strategic planning. Without a blink I took a 15 percent pay cut partly because of my severance package and partly because I was already looking for real estate investments. Also, this job was a lot less stressful than the one at Sony. Even better, travel wasn't required.

Between October and November 2001 I did something I had never done before. I set up a line of credit. I read other books by Robert and played CASHFLOW 101 with like-minded friends.

I also began looking for rental properties in Texas on the Internet. San Antonio was particularly appealing because my sister-in-law lives there, and she agreed to manage the properties I bought.

By December 2001 two duplexes were chosen and I closed on them both in January 2002. My new life had begun.

During this new period of my life an amazing transformation began to take place. Much to my amazement and delight, fear became an unexpected ally instead of remaining an old enemy. In the past I felt too scared, too lacking in confidence in my ability to analyze and act where my financial situation was concerned. Now fear helped me make progress because I recognized that I could change my financial future. Whenever I felt the taunting presence of fear, I reviewed the essential concepts I learned from Robert. I took the time necessary to compare my progress with my goals. That way I reaffirmed my ability to make sound decisions and execute my plans.

Fear had functioned as the obstacle that held me back my entire adulthood. While the fear didn't completely disappear—I don't think that's possible—it did morph into an energy source that helped me to take action.

Here's How I Did It

First, I took a giant step backward in order to fully assess and identify my near-term (one-, two-, and three-year) and long-range (five- and ten-year) objectives. Prior to this I had only done a cursory assessment, which proved to have one key thing missing, which I think is common to most folks just starting out. That is, if I planned to use OPM (other people's money), then I not only had to take the debt servicing of the mortgage into account but also the debt servicing for any ancillary funds (such as down payments).

For example, if I used OPM for both down payments and mortgages, which meant not tapping into any of my own cash for an acquisition, I had to factor this into the equation for cashflow. I wanted each property to be fully cash-positive in every aspect, paying for itself 100 percent in addition to providing me with passive income. I didn't want any surprises, or missed or hidden expenses—and the fact was that I embraced using OPM wholeheartedly.

The next major realization I had was that my cashflow had to reflect increases in my existing expenses over time. Inflation, more expensive health care—expenses always rose during a "normal" retirement process. Retiring from the rat race was no different. I couldn't just evaluate the cashflow of the property. While the real estate may have been able to pay for itself, if it wasn't paying my noninvestment expenses as well, then I'd need to keep working. That would mean ending up doing two jobs either forever or until I figured out the mistake or I got fed up and pulled out of real estate. I reckoned that if my normal monthly expenses were $5,000 (primary home mortgage, insurance, cable, phone, newspaper, food, dining out, car, and so forth), then the cashflow from my real estate investments had to reflect this factor.

So I put together a model, about 60 percent of which I developed during the first three months that I actively looked at and evaluated property. The remaining 40 percent was refined when I purchased my first two properties. I've found that a lot of people tend to think in terms of traditional real estate expenses (i.e., the type of costs incurred as a home owner), which are different from expenses associated with investment real estate. Consequently, my model included distribution of expenses based on region for "cross-property" expenses such as legal fees and travel costs. It also built in a combination of monthly, annual, and ten-year expenses in order to establish an accurate budget.

Expenses included insurance, taxes, home warranty costs, initial make-ready for long-term tenant transition, property management fees (monthly/per lease and lease renewal), advertisements, yard maintenance, electricity/water/waste removal charges, homeowners association dues, travel expenses to and from the city based on two trips per year, and attorney services. Then I factored in ten-year expenses such as roof replacement, appliance replacement, exterior painting, and other things that tend to happen once in the time frame of owning the property (this also depended on my exit strategy, that is, when I planned to sell). I believe not taking all these expenses into account is the first mistake that new investors make, and therefore sours them on real estate as an investment.

The model I used was deliberately a worst-case scenario because my assumption was that best cases seldom ever happened and definitely never in the first year of acquisition. By using a worst-case analysis my model enabled me to be 99.99 percent sure that I would get positive cashflow from day one of purchase even if vacancies were high, the cost of initial acquisition was elevated (for instance, if preliminary make-ready repairs were needed after purchase), and so on. This allowed a good degree of flexibility in factors that were always variable while still generating positive cashflow.

The model also helped to eliminate the emotional investment factor that can come into play, particularly early in the learning process for new investors. I didn't even look at a property until I ran it through the model to first determine if it met my financial objectives. I walked away from many properties because they did not fit into my paradigm.

I saw the first four properties prior to making an offer. The next two properties I did not see in person until after I had a sales contract on them. However, I asked a friend in the area to do a brief drive-by to scout the location and appearance. The most recent property was bought basically sight unseen, based on a drive-by of a friend and a photo from the seller. I personally believe that distance helps to minimize or eliminate problems associated with broker or agent pressure to sign on the spot as well as emotional attachment to a property. (Distance forces one to do the numbers first. And remember that the terms of the sales contract *always* include a clause enabling the buyer to terminate the deal. The termination can be related to inspections, lending arrangements, and/or just a general opt-out clause in exchange for some nominal fee to the seller like $50 on a $150,000 property.)

Additionally, my model permitted me to turn down a property when dealing with real estate agents or brokers, thus avoiding the hard-sell exploitation that is commonly experienced by new investors.

I used two methods to determine cashflow. One was a proprietary spreadsheet I created that includes all anticipated expenses. The other was an off-the-shelf product, which I used to confirm and validate assumptions (basically, I employed this as an objective expert view and review of my personal analysis, sort of like a system of checks and balances).

For the first property I purchased, I evaluated seven lenders including online mortgage brokers. Closing costs were a factor of the lending relationship. Again, my model included a checklist in order to compare basic rates and closing costs as well as loan structure. Five of the properties I purchased had all expenses paid by the seller for repairs needed prior to changing owners based on negotiation of the sales contract. Two of the properties were purchased as is and needed approximately $3,000 per duplex in repairs. I paid for them, but since they were included in the mortgage amount, no out-of-pocket expenses were required at the closing.

Best of all, the model allowed me to make a decision on a property within minutes. This was important to me because I wanted to be as aggressive as possible and acquire lucrative properties quickly and efficiently.

An initial phone call was all that was required to ask important questions. I could evaluate as many as fifteen to twenty properties in a single day anywhere in the world without having to leave home. This became particularly important when I came across a new hidden gem. I have made offers in less than thirty minutes after a property has been listed. In two of those cases, I now own the properties and the cashflow is positive for both.

I used a checklist template that helped me to quickly select and fill out answers during my initial phone conversation. The list included: size, layout (study, separate laundry room, attached/detached garage), number of full/partial bathrooms, family room, living room, separate dining room, style of kitchen, separate foyer, roof age (in years), foundation, construction (frame, brick), air conditioning and type, heating and type, utility, and whether there was a fireplace. Proximity to schools and shopping, access to public transportation and distance from major roadways, and whether the property was adjacent to a vacant lot were noted as well.

The last sale date (some states limit the information about previous sales), prior purchase price, previous appraisal price, number of units per property, average occupancy, whether the property was fully rented currently, the rent rolls, and the anniversary for lease renewals completed the inventory. It may sound like a lot, but I could get through this list in combination with information from the MLS (multiple listing service) and public records in the county tax office via the Internet in under fifteen minutes.

I also put together a checklist of activities that needed to be performed (and their order if appropriate). This outlined who did what, which helped to ensure that I had a consistent purchase methodology and that nothing got lost in the shuffle. Doing so saved my bacon numerous times on deals in which I worked directly with the seller as well as deals involving agents and brokers. In my experience, I've found that deals involving agents and brokers are the most prone to having forgotten steps, since the buyer normally expects the agent to be on top of this stuff. I've found this to be an incorrect assumption, which is why my model includes the steps in a checklist format that makes it easy to identify what has been done and what is still left to do. As a result, the closing becomes almost a nonevent. It is also an effective tool for negotiations because some agents are greener than they appear. As a buyer I can propose items during the negotiation that work to my advantage (but translate into a smaller commission for the agents involved).

Finally, the model contains some standard assessments that a lender would do to qualify a buyer for a loan as well as typical things like cash-on-cash return, annual depreciation, and so forth.

By the way, I've observed a lot of people descend into a feeding frenzy due to perceived lack of progress. For every one property I've purchased I looked at approximately thirty to forty possibilities. I know that there is a tendency to get frustrated with the process early on, which often leads to making a decision to buy based on panic rather than evaluation and qualification. "Why can't I locate good properties?" or "Why haven't I bought anything yet?" are complaints I've heard a lot. Time and patience to locate and evaluate properties are part of the process.

I should also mention that I am not, nor have I ever been, a professional real estate agent or broker. My background is mainly high-tech, and I was lousy in math at school. If I can do it, anybody with an interest in real estate and patience with the process can, too.

My Properties

The price range for all my properties to date runs between $115,000 and $180,000. All were below the seller's initial requested sales price due to heavy negotiation, which included expenses paid by the seller for transfer repairs (things like new water heaters and roofing repairs). Five of the properties had equity at closing, which I used to pay expenses or buy additional property.

Based on the model I use and the structure of the mortgages, one unit out of a two-unit duplex (or two units out of a four-plex) will pay mortgage/insurance/home warranty/taxes. I include a monthly expense budget equivalent to about $100 per two units in one duplex and $200 for four units within a four-plex.

My sister-in-law still manages all the San Antonio properties, and a friend who lives Fresno, California, handles the property I own there. I reached agreements with both that allow them to learn the business of property management and investment while permitting me some flexibility in compensation. They both get paid but at rates lower than a professional property manager since they are just now learning the business. As their knowledge and experience grows, so will their compensation. I plan to include both in future partnership-type property deals once I feel they've acquired a good baseline knowledge. In effect, I am able to "share the wealth" not just financially, but professionally as well as they both begin new careers.

However, my analysis always includes standard rates for the property manager in case I ever need to use these services either at the close or at a later date. Since my current inventory is two to four units per property, I use the typical 10 percent of monthly rents collected, along with half a month's rent for a new tenant/lease (and assuming at least one new tenant a year per unit). Management fees for commercial property, such as a fifty-unit apartment complex, are based on a different fee rate and schedule. I plan to use a model of compensation that will encourage the property manager to retain good tenants, eliminate trouble spots, and ensure no deferred maintenance.

Currently I own seven multifamily properties. From the day I bought them they spun off cashflow. They also have lots of appreciation potential. Here are the cashflow numbers from January 2001 through November 2002 (nine months) for the first six properties. The date above each column is the month of acquisition.

AR = accounts receivable (payments paid to me, that is, rents received from tenants).

AP = accounts payable (payments paid by me, including mortgages, taxes, insurance, maintenance fees, and other expenses).

| Jan 2002 | Jan 2002 | Mar 2002 | Mar 2002 | Sep 2002 | Oct 2002 |
| Duplex 1 | Duplex 2 | Duplex 3 | Duplex 4 | Duplex 5 | Duplex 6 |

Subtotal AR

| $15,440.00 | $14,465.00 | $11,200.00 | $12,800.00 | $3,545.00 | $2,000.00 |

Grand total AR	$59,450.00
Grand total AP	$17,595.12
Grand total cashflow	$41,854.88

Here's the breakdown for one duplex:

Purchase price: $162,000

Cash put into property

Down payment:	$25,000
Closing costs paid by me:	$2,100
Repairs paid by me:	$1,500
	$28,600

Monthly cashflow analysis

Rental income (both units of this duplex): $2,000

(This property has had a 100% occupancy rate to date, so while I normally factor in a 5% vacancy loss I didn't include it here.)

Monthly expenses

—Taxes (property):	$304
—Insurance:	$54
—Repairs/maintenance:	$0
—Reserve:	$175

(Similar to the management fee weighting, I assume that certain repairs/expenses will occur annually and every ten years. To date for this property, actual monthly expenses in the past seven months have been $0. However, the budgeted weighted-average expenses run $175 a month for both units of this one duplex, which gets put into an interest-bearing account. The expenses include the homeowners association dues and make-ready, like painting, cleaning, and so on.

–Management fee: $141.67

(For this specific property, the fee runs 5% of total collected rents = $100 per month plus an additional 25% of the first month's rent for make-ready/new lease execution = $500 per year based on an annual new lease factor. I assume at least one new lease per unit every year, which is a worst-case scenario. The weighted management fee monthly runs $141.67 = $1,200+$500÷12. The extra funds get put into a repair CD to collect interest until and if needed.)

–Loan payment (5-year ARM, 30 years at 4.598%):	$535.97
	$1,210.64
Net monthly cashflow:	$789.36

Cash-on-cash return

Annual cashflow ($789.36 × 12)	$ 9,472.32
÷	
Amount of cash put into property	$28,600
Cash-on-cash return	33%

In 2003, the appraised value of the property was $169,000.

Here's something to keep in mind: Estimated cashflow made prior to property acquisition and based on information from the seller and other sources is almost never equal to actual cashflow. Some expenses are higher, like taxes and make-ready. Other expenses, like monthly repairs, may be lower.

The Journey of a Year

Since September 2001 I have doubled my net worth by investing in real estate and recovered the nearly three quarters of a million dollars I lost in the stock market. And where the stock market was concerned I learned the importance of actively analyzing stocks and reaching my own decisions. This was a major departure from the past, when I relied solely on the advice of a broker. The method of stock acquisition and management that I now use has grown the worth of my portfolio 20 percent since September 2001. Not only do I depend on myself, I respect the decisions I make. I give credit to the CASHFLOW 101 game, which helped me to adjust my mind-set and perspective. Explicitly getting "near-real life experience" with my own decision process that I would refine and take from the game into real life, I was able to view and structure deals creatively—and to my advantage.

Within six months of buying property I paid off $30,000 in credit card debt. Today I'm close to tripling my net worth.

In the next year I plan to switch from small deals to big deals, a mix of real estate and businesses with a minimum of $1 million in capital gains per deal. These will involve limited partnerships with two or three other people I know very well. These transactions will be financed using equity earned in past deals. Leveraging what I did in the past creates momentum for the future. I'll do that for three to five years. At the end of that period I will transition to the fast track. Here are my goals:

- By March 2003 my net worth will be greater than $800,000.
- By March 2004 my net worth will be greater than $2 million. I will retire from my day job.
- By March 2006 my net worth will be greater than $5 million—and this is the worst-case outlook.

The First Steps Are the Hardest

Because it is in direct opposition to everything my parents taught me about money, learning how to correctly use other people's money was, for me, the hardest part of using the Rich Dad information. But it was balanced by the easiest part for me, which is the straight language and methods that conveyed what I needed to know. To aid me, I put together a team of advisors who provide me with the information and knowledge I require to make decisions and act on them. Every person was a referral and each one understands my vision.

I've also formulated by own equation for success. Success = one part knowledge (lessons learned) + one part information (lessons learned by others that are shared) + risk (value and potential gain compared to worst case and potential loss). This includes the potential loss of opportunity as well, which means considering what I stand to lose by *not* taking the risk. I believe that risk is the one manageable component in the total success equation, whether that achievement is financial, personal, or anything else.

Taking these risks gave me such a surge of empowerment that I decided to take other steps. The more I accomplished, the more confidence I gained. I possessed a deep well of self-assurance that I was able to use in ways I hadn't thought. After I closed my first real estate deal I practically levitated with elation.

Afterward, I tapped into that well to succeed in a totally unrelated area. Like many people my age, I had been putting on weight for years. All that time sitting on planes coupled with lack of exercise and a lot of business dinners took their toll. Eventually I was carrying sixty extra pounds and my doctor warned me that I was in danger of having a stroke.

Asking myself what I could lose—so to speak—I used my newly discovered self-assurance to set realistic goals and execute weight loss plans. I'm proud to say that twelve months after taking charge of my body I was sixty pounds lighter. How cool is this: Robert's concepts don't just change your mind—they change your body!

The Future Beckons

I often think about how I transformed my life in one year.

On September 10, 2001, I was overweight and depressed about my spiraling-down financial situation. I felt locked in the "golden handcuffs" of a high-level corporate career without the possibility of parole.

On September 11, 2001, I survived a cataclysmic event and found the means to pull myself out of my stupor.

Today I feel like I've climbed from the devastation of Ground Zero to the top of a majestic mountain. The air is so clear I can see for miles and miles. Opportunities beckon in every direction.

They are waiting for you, too. Go and find them.

Someday is right now.

Robert Kiyosaki

Born and raised in Hawaii, Robert Kiyosaki is a fourth-generation Japanese-American. After graduating from college in New York, Robert joined the Marine Corps and served in Vietnam as an officer and helicopter gunship pilot. Following the war, Robert worked for the Xerox Corporation in sales. In 1977, he started a company that brought the first nylon Velcro 'surfer wallets' to market. And in 1985 he founded an international education company that taught business and investing to tens of thousands of students throughout the world.

In 1994, Robert sold his business and retired at the age of 47.

During his short-lived retirement, Robert, in collaboration with co-author Sharon Lechter, his CPA and business partner, wrote the book *Rich Dad Poor Dad*. Soon after he wrote *Rich Dad's CASHFLOW Quadrant, Rich Dad's Guide to Investing, Rich Kid Smart Kid, Retire Young Retire Rich, Rich Dad's Prophecy* – all of which earned spots on the bestseller lists of the *Wall Street Journal, Business Week, New York Times,* E-Trade.com, Amazon.com and others.

Prior to becoming a best-selling author, Robert created an educational board game – CASHFLOW 101 – to teach individuals the financial strategies that his Rich Dad spent years teaching him. It was those financial strategies that allowed Robert to retire at the age of 47.

In 2001, the first of the series of Rich Dad's Advisors books was launched. This team of professionals supports Robert's belief that "business and investing are team sports."

In Robert's words: "We go to school to learn to work hard for money. I write books and create products that teach people how to have money work hard for them. Then they can enjoy the luxuries of this great world we live in."

Rich Dad's Organization is the collaborative effort of Robert and Kim Kiyosaki and Sharon Lechter, who, in 1996, embarked on a journey that would afford them the opportunity to impact the financial literacy of people everywhere and carry the Rich Dad mission to every corner of the world.

Sharon Lechter

CPA, co-author of the Rich Dad series of books and CEO of the Rich Dad Organization, Sharon Lechter had dedicated her professional efforts to the field of education. She graduated with honors from Florida State University with a degree in accounting, then joined the ranks of Coopers & Lybrand, a Big Eight accounting firm. Sharon held various management positions with computer, insurance, and publishing companies while maintaining her professional credentials as a CPA.

Sharon and husband, Michael Lechter, have been married for over twenty years and are parents to three children, Phillip, Shelly and William. As her children grew, she became actively involved in their education and served in leadership positions in their schools. She became a vocal activist in the areas of mathematics, computers, reading, and writing education.

In 1989, she joined forces with the inventor of the first electronic "talking book" and helped him expand the electronic book industry to a multimillion dollar international market.

Today she remains a pioneer in developing new technologies to bring education into children's lives in ways that are innovative, challenging, and fun. As co-author of the Rich Dad books and CEO of that company, she focuses her efforts in the arena of financial education.

"Our current educational system has not been able to keep pace with the global and technological changes in the world today," Sharon states. "We must teach our young people the skills – both scholastic and financial – that they need to not only survive but to flourish in the world."

A committed philanthropist, Sharon "gives back" to the world communities as both a volunteer and a benefactor. She directs the Foundation for Financial Literacy and is a strong advocate of education and the need for improved financial literacy.

Sharon and Michael were honored by Childhelp USA, a national organization founded to eradicate child abuse in the United States, as recipients of the 2002 "Spirit of the Children" Award. And, in May of 2002, Sharon was named chairman of the board for the Phoenix chapter of Childhelp USA.

As an active member of Women's Presidents Organization, she enjoys networking with other professional women across the country.

Robert Kiyosaki, her business partner and friend, says "Sharon is one of the few natural entrepreneurs I have ever met. My respect for her continues to grow every day that we work together."

Rich Dad's Organization is the collaborative effort of Robert and Kim Kiyosaki and Sharon Lechter, who, in 1996, embarked on a journey that would afford them the opportunity to impact the financial literacy of people everywhere and carry the Rich Dad mission to every corner of the world.

Robert Kiyosaki's Edumercial
An Educational Commercial

The Three Incomes

In the world of accounting, there are three different types of income: earned, passive and portfolio. When my real dad said to me, "Go to school, get good grades and find a safe secure job," he was recommending I work for earned income. When my rich dad said, "The rich don't work for money, they have their money work for them," he was talking about passive income and portfolio income. Passive income, in most cases, is derived from real estate investments. Portfolio income is income derived from paper assets, such as stocks, bonds, and mutual funds.

Rich dad used to say, "The key to becoming wealthy is the ability to convert earned income into passive income and/or portfolio income as quickly as possible." He would say, "The taxes are highest on earned income. The least taxed income is passive income. That is another reason why you want your money working hard for you. The government taxes the income you work hard for more than the income your money works hard for."

The Key to Financial Freedom

The key to financial freedom and great wealth is a person's ability or skill to convert earned income into passive income and/or portfolio income. That is the skill that my rich dad spent a lot of time teaching Mike and me. Having that skill is the reason my wife Kim and I are financially free, never needing to work again. We continue to work because we choose to. Today we own a real estate investment company for passive income and participate in private placements and initial public offerings of stock for portfolio income.

Investing to become rich requires a different set of personal skills – skills essential for financial success as well as low-risk and high-investment returns. In other words, knowing how to create assets that buy other assets. The problem is that gaining the basic education and experience required is often time consuming, frightening, and expensive, especially when you make mistakes with your own money. That is why I created the patented education board games trademarked as CASHFLOW®.

Rich Dad Poor Dad

What the rich teach their kids about money that the poor and middle class do not. Learn how to have your money work for you and why you don't need to earn a high income to be rich.

The book that "rocked" the financial world.

J.P. Morgan declares "Rich Dad Poor Dad a must-read for Millionaires."
The Wall Street Journal

"A starting point for anyone looking to gain control of their financial future."
USA Today

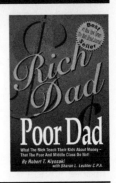

Rich Dad's CASHFLOW Quadrant

Rich Dad's guide to financial freedom. Learn about the four CASHFLOW Quadrants and you will understand the most important keys to creating wealth.

The sequel to Rich Dad Poor Dad, Rich Dad's Cashflow Quadrant describes the four types of people who make up the world of business and the core value differences between them. It discusses the tools an individual needs to become a successful business owner and investor.

Rich Dad's Guide to Investing

What the rich invest in that the poor and middle class do not. Learn how you can apply the techniques of the rich to create your own wealth and have it grow.

This is the third book in the Rich Dad Series. Rich Dad's Guide to Investing discusses what the rich invest in that the poor and middle class do not. Robert provides an insider's look into the world of investing, how the rich find the best investments, and how you can apply the techniques of the rich to create your own wealth.

Rich Dad's Rich Kid Smart Kid

Give your child a financial headstart. Awaken your child's love of learning how to be financially free. Imagine the results you'll see when they start early!

This book is written for parents who value education, want to give their child a financial and academic headstart in life, and are willing to take an active role to make it happen. Rich Kid Smart Kid is designed to help you give your child the same inspiring and practical financial knowledge that Robert's rich dad gave him. Learn how to awaken your child's love of learning.

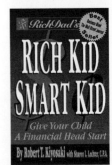

Rich Dad's Retire Young Retire Rich

A powerful personal story about how Robert and Kim Kiyosaki started with nothing, and retired financially free in less than 10 years. If you do not plan on working hard all your life, this book is for you.

If you're tired of the same old investment advice — such as "be patient," "invest for the long term," and "diversify" — then this book is for you.

Robert explains in detail the power of leverage. How to leverage your mind, your financial plans, your actions and most importantly, your first steps to becoming financially free.

You will learn Rich Dad's techniques using leverage to first build financial security and ultimately have the life you want.

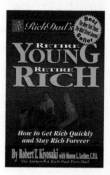

Rich Dad's Prophecy

Why the Biggest Stock Market Crash in History Is Still Coming...and How You Can Prepare Yourself and Profit from It!

In the 6th book of the Rich Dad Series, Robert Kiyosaki predicts the inevitable financial crisis that will hit the U.S. when 83 million baby boomers retire, taking with them such a vast amount of savings that the market is sure to crumble. And that doesn't even take into account the already wobbly state of the stock market, as blue chip companies go under, sending the Dow plummeting. But Rich Dad's Prophecy is not a "doom and gloom" book, it's a "doom and boom" book, with sure-fire strategies designed to avoid disaster in the coming crisis.

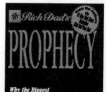

Rich Dad's Success Stories

Learn why you're never too young to achieve financial success and read the many stories from people of all ages. Each story is inspiring because instead of people now feeling entitled to have money handed to them, they are setting goals, achieving them and creating income — they are learning to take control of their lives. This book is about real life people who followed the Rich Dad lessons to take control of their financial lives.

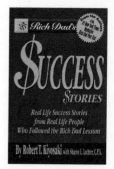

CASHFLOW® 101

CASHFLOW 101 is an educational program that teaches accounting, finance, and investing at the same time...and makes learning fun.

Learn how to get out of the rat race and onto the fast track where your money works for you instead of you working hard for your money. The educational program, CASHFLOW 101, includes three audiocassettes which reveal distinctions on CASHFLOW 101 as well as valuable investment information and a video titled "The Secrets of the Rich."

CASHFLOW 101 is recommended for adults and children age 10 and older.

CASHFLOW® 202

CASHFLOW 202 teaches you the advanced business and investing techniques used by technical investors by adding volatility to the game. It teaches the advanced investment techniques of "short-selling stock," "put-options," "call-options," "straddles" and real estate exchanges.

You must have CASHFLOW 101 in order to play CASHFLOW 202. This package contains new game sheets, new playing cards, and four audiocassettes.

CASHFLOW for KIDS™

Give your children the financial headstart necessary to thrive in today's fast-paced and changing world. Schools teach children how to work for money. CASHFLOW for Kids teaches children how to have money work for them.

CASHFLOW for Kids is a complete educational package which includes the book and audiocassette titled "Rich Dad's Guide to Raising Your Child's Financial I.Q."

CASHFLOW for Kids is recommended for children ages 6 and older.

Protecting Your #1 Asset – Creating Fortunes From Your Ideas
An Intellectual Property Handbook

Protecting your #1 Asset will teach you how to turn your ideas into intellectual property assets, avoid inadvertently giving away your rights, use intellectual property to build barriers to competition and generate cash flow by licensing your intellectual property to others.

by Michael Lechter, Esq.

Sales Dogs – You Do Not Have To Be An Attack Dog To Be Successful In Sales

Sales Dogs will introduce five breeds of Sales Dogs which will allow you to make more money by playing to your natural strengths. It reveal the five simple but critical revenue-generating skills to create endless streams of qualified buyers and life-long sales, and teaches you how to radically change your attitude in 30 seconds or less so you can direct your financial results.

by Blair Singer

LoopHoles Of The Rich – How The Rich Legally Make More Money And Pay Less Taxes

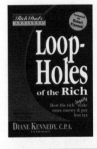

LoopHoles of the Rich reveals how to control how much tax you pay and when you pay it, and condenses 500,000+ pages of IRS Tax law into three easy rules that keep money in your pocket. It also shows you how to find the right business structure for your business to pay less tax and protect what you have.

by Diane Kennedy, C.P.A.

Own Your Own Corporation – Why The Rich Own Their Own Companies And Everyone Else Works For Them

Own Your Own Corporation illustrates how to:

- Select the best entity for your own personal strategy
- Raise money for your new venture
- Maximize the incredible benefits of a C corporation
- Use employment agreements for your benefit
- Use Nevada corporations for asset protection and tax savings
- Easily prepare and maintain corporate records

by Garrett Sutton, Esq.

Real Estate Riches – How To Become Rich Using Your Banker's Money

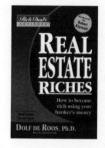

Real Estate Riches will:
- Show you why real estate is tens and hundreds of times better than other investments
- Train you how to find the "Deal of the Decade" – every week
- Teach you how to massively increase the value of a property without spending much money
- Explain how the tax man can subsidize your real estate investment
- Reveal how to create passive income using your banker's money so that you only work if you want to

by Dolf de Roos, Ph.D.

How To Buy And Sell A Business – How You Can Win In The Business Quadrant

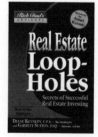

How To Buy And Sell A Business reveals the strategies used by successful entrepreneurs to acquire and cash out business investments. Written in a clear and easily understandable style, How To Buy And Sell A Business provides the necessary knowledge to avoid the pitfalls and overcome the obstacles in order to achieve a winning transaction.

by Garrett Sutton, Esq.

Real Estate LoopHoles – Secrets Of Successful Real Estate Investing

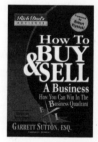

Real Estate LoopHoles will reveal how to use tax loopholes to your advantage and stop others from using legal loopholes to take your assets. In addition, you will learn to:
- Determine the best way to hold title to your real estate investments
- Use your own home as a tax-free, money-making venture
- Use the Seven Tax Loopholes only available to real estate owners
- Protect your real estate assets from tenants and creditors

by Diane Kennedy, C.P.A. and Garrett Sutton, Esq.